Praise for

HEAVY LIFTING:

BUILDING A BUSINESS WITH A GIANT HEART

Larry O'Toole and I may have run very different companies, but we are leadership kindred spirits. Just as my book is titled ***It's Not About the Coffee****, Larry's* ***Heavy Lifting: Building a Business With a Giant Heart*** *isn't about the moving. We both recognize that if you grow your people, you'll grow your business; that if you connect with your customer as a human being, they'll keep coming back; and that your guiding principles (and how you stick to them) determine the kind of leader and organization you are. Just as* ***The Green Apron Book*** *was pivotal in establishing and maintaining Starbucks's unique culture, the success of Gentle Giant proves what having a giant HEART can do.*

I had the honor of leading Starbucks from a small group of committed individuals to a much larger one, and I know firsthand the wide gap between the wisdom of knowing what's right and the wisdom to do what's right. As readers will see in story after story, Larry, too, is the rare leader who possesses the wisdom to do what's right. ***Heavy Lifting*** *is a testament to leading with integrity and courage.*

I truly believe we're all responsible for leading ourselves to realize our potential and to make the greatest possible contribution to work and the world around us. I greatly enjoyed reading ***Heavy Lifting*** *and highly recommend it to anyone aspiring to or currently running a business, leaders (both with a capital L and a lowercase l, which is everyone), and to anyone in need of a genuinely moving story.*

—**Howard Behar**, former president of Starbucks Coffee Company North America and Starbucks Coffee International and author of ***It's Not About the Coffee: Lessons on Putting People First from a Life at Starbucks***

Heavy Lifting

To request permissions, contact the author at
lotoole@gentlegiant.com

Cover art and book layout by Larry O'Toole
with Cindy Murphy, Bluemoon Graphics.

Published by Priory Grove Publishing

ISBN 979-8-9955088-0-9

Heavy Lifting

Building a Business With a Giant Heart

Larry O'Toole

To my parents, James Davitt Bermingham O'Toole and Elizabeth (Betty) Ryan O'Toole, who continuously modeled integrity and courage.

TABLE OF CONTENTS

"If you grow people, the people grow the business."

—Howard Behar, former president of
Starbucks Coffee Company North America
and Starbucks Coffee International and author of
*It's Not About the Coffee: Lessons on Putting People First
from a Life at Starbucks*

Preamble

By the time we decided we should have a written statement of our core values, Gentle Giant Moving Company was already thriving with a culture of excellence and a shared sense of purpose. Everyone was asked to submit in writing their view of the company's five most important operating principles. The submissions received were strikingly well aligned. Consensus quickly emerged:

Honesty. No one who works for Gentle Giant should ever lie to a customer, another employee, or anyone else.

Enthusiasm. Employees should demonstrate that they want to be there, on the job, and to attack the work with energy.

Above and Beyond. Giants will go the extra mile to make the customer happy.

Respect. Our people are polite and considerate—always—to customers, to each other, and to everyone they interact with.

Teamwork. Employees are there for each other: backing up their colleagues and helping them succeed.

Run your eyes down the first letters of those words and you'll see that our values create the acronym HEART. That outcome, fortunately, required very little linguistic massaging. No mnemonics are required. HEART, which we now routinely refer to as the Giant HEART, is at once apt and elegant. Team members have only to conjure the word to know what to do in any given situation.

I wrote this book to tell the story of building a successful company on these core values. My hope is that readers will glean some useful advice, have their hearts touched, and their spirits lifted.

Foreword

Leading with Heart, Building with Purpose

In a world where industries differ but human values remain constant, this book tells a story that transcends the boundaries of business categories. What began as a personal and professional journey to build a world-class moving company has evolved into a blueprint for leadership, character development, and organizational excellence.

The ten chapters ahead are rooted in the real-world experiences of Gentle Giant Moving Company, a business renowned not only for its operational success, but for its unwavering commitment to people, principles, and purpose. While the setting is the moving industry, the lessons apply to any field where teams must collaborate, trust must be earned, and excellence must be pursued.

This is not just a book about building a business. It is a book about building people.

From cultivating a values-driven culture (Chapter 3: Finding Giants with HEART) to mastering the art of customer service (Chapter 5), and from overcoming adversity with integrity (Chapter 8) to empowering durable purpose-driven leadership (Chapter 9), the journey outlined here offers insights relevant to educators, entrepreneurs, nonprofit leaders, athletes, managers, and anyone committed to making a meaningful impact.

What makes this book especially resonant is the voice behind it, Larry O'Toole. Larry's warm, authentic storytelling brings each lesson to life with the ease and charm of a fireside chat. His gift lies in transforming everyday business scenarios into memorable narratives that reveal deeper truths about character, community, and the human spirit. His stories don't just inform, they connect, inspire, and stay with you long after the final page.

Each chapter provides a lens into how seemingly simple ideas—Honesty, Enthusiasm, Above and Beyond, Respect, and Teamwork—can create extraordinary results when authentically lived. Whether you're leading a classroom, running a startup, managing a global team, or simply seeking to grow as an individual, this book offers practical inspiration for leading with HEART, navigating challenges, and building enduring success.

Welcome to the story of Gentle Giant. May it help you write your own.

Deborah McGonigle
Former Fortune 100 Executive

CHAPTER ONE

How Gentle Giant Came to Be

Here's one of the great things about being a mover. You can always tell a moving story.

There is a pub called The Muddy Charles on the MIT campus in Cambridge, Massachusetts. Back in the '80s, when Gentle Giant was still a small, scrappy business renting space from the university, our movers would congregate there after long, thirsty days spent hauling people's lives across the city. Tossing back beers at wooden tables before a massive fireplace engraved in Latin, they would hold court, trying to one-up each other's stories. Now, more than forty years later, with our movers located in many different states, they still delight in trying to top a story.

Some of those stories are brags, like the guy boasting about a job in Back Bay where his crew moved so fast that a crowd gathered to watch and cheer them on. (He passed out business cards, of course.) Others are tales of Herculean efforts, such as the description of a fourth-floor walk-up in Boston's North End on a humid day that hit 95 degrees. By the end, the crew chief swore that the crew's sweat was pouring down the stairs.

Then there are all the stories about amusing eccentrics—the hoarders, the screamers, the micromanagers, and the frantic. We had to rescue one customer who had become trapped in a broken-down elevator. One family asked us to move their grandmother, still in her bed, into the back of a truck. One customer had us move a giant boulder. (He had a sentimental reason.) One of our movers had to wash and pack eight sets of expensive China dishes stacked higher than the windows over the sink. One of our crews packed and moved a home strewn with mouse traps, some of which had occupants. One mouse had drowned in a bottle of Châteauneuf-du-Pape.

Truly, there is no work like moving to test a person's mettle. The physical labor is grueling. Many times, we've had to haul stuff up and down the stairs of a high rise when the elevator was out. We have moved households that held a library's worth of books, and with every book box weighing about 40 pounds, that's a lot of heavy lifting. Pianos and equipment, such as metalworking machines, may weigh 800 pounds or more. Or imagine moving a massive, six-foot-tall safe that felt like it was full of gold bricks up the stairs of a five-story condominium. Then imagine finding out that all it held was five championship rings—prize possessions for a part-owner of the (then ABA) New Jersey Nets.

We have moved people in triple-digit heat. We have moved people in the middle of snowstorms. We have moved people during power outages by candlelight without an elevator. Moving jobs can present a head spinning combination of physical, logistical, mathematical, meteorological, engineering, and psychological challenges on any given day.

Our movers always try to make things easy on customers. They want to transform what most consider an ordeal into a good day—even a fun one. And most of our customers are kind and endlessly grateful.

How a job goes isn't determined by the furniture, the weather, or the number of staircases—it is determined by whether we have won the customer's heart.

Irish Beginnings

In the early years, the character of an entrepreneurial company is shaped in large part by its founder. And the founder's character is shaped by the people who raised him. So, let's start with my family, back in Ireland. A cerebral lot—both literary and science-minded—they didn't set me on the path to build a business. But their values, in many ways, influenced the kind of business I would build.

My father, James O'Toole, was many things: an engineer, an editor, a playwright, and a radio and TV commentator. First and foremost, though, he was a principled idealist. Raised in Shanghai by strict, exceedingly demanding parents, he believed in hard work, honesty, respect, and giving people the benefit of the doubt. When faced with a fight—so long as it was a good fight—he never backed down. He resisted hypocrisy and corruption.

Opening Night at Man Alive

That spirit underlies one of the O'Toole family's more famous bits of lore. While employed by the Electric Supply Board, Ireland's electric utility, my father wrote a play that caused a whirlwind of controversy at its 1961 Dublin debut. *Man Alive* satirized a particular type of feckless bureaucracy: state-owned enterprises like the very one my father worked for. Although the play was written about the dehumanizing effects of bureaucratic hierarchies in general, the Electric Supply Board management, perhaps predictably, decided it reflected badly on them, and were not amused. The utility managed to halt production after full dress rehearsals at both the Abbey Theatre and the Gate Theatre. But the bureaucrats failed at their third attempt to stop the show, at the Olympia Theatre, to my father's great delight.

Man Alive is the story of an idealistic everyman who just wants to excel at his job. But his superiors resent him, particularly his insistence on excellence and accountability. The resentment manifests most visibly in attempts to silence and intimidate with poor (and secret) performance reviews. He decides to fight back. And though he doesn't win the war, he wins the battle, standing up to workplace injustice and holding onto his job and integrity to the end. "As long as I stay, I'll be a thorn in their backside," he asserts at the end of the play. "And every time they sit on anyone again, they'll think of me."

My father had worked on *Man Alive* for many years before it was produced. The play was discussed so much in our household that, when I was five, I carved the title into our mahogany dining room table with scissors. The desecration wasn't visible beneath the lace tablecloth, and my parents didn't discover it until weeks later. When I got home from school, I overheard them discussing whether this would be the first time that corporal punishment would be an appropriate response to my transgressions. To my great relief, their loving nature won out, and the long, serious talk they had with me definitely convinced me to treat all furniture with nothing but appreciation and care from that day onward. Little did they know that they were preparing me for a career protecting fine antiques.

On being informed of this incident, my grandmother was horrified at my parents' total lack of judgment. Why on earth would they want to raise a juvenile delinquent? It was of the utmost importance that I be beaten for this terrible crime against mahogany, and so she headed for my school to inform my teacher. She let him know that my fate was in his hands, and he would have to pick up the slack. He, a Christian

Brother, was a man who approached corporal punishment as though it were an Olympic event. He called me out in front of the whole class for damaging the table. He then ordered me to the front where he wailed on me with a leather strap. He gave me "12 of the best" on each hand.

Despite those best efforts, my gentle nature survived. The loving and reasoned reaction of my parents had taught me everything I needed to know. Years later, when I heard the expression "you get more with honey than with vinegar," I knew exactly what it meant. Today that is a phrase often heard around Gentle Giant.

I was 10 years old when I finally saw *Man Alive* performed. It was a revelation. For the first time, I understood that the playing field is tilted toward wealth and power. If anything is going to change for the better, it is both dangerous and necessary for little guys to make big noises. I admired the courage and integrity of the play's protagonist. My father's courage and integrity as he resisted his employer's pressure was not lost on me.

Decades later, my sister Margot followed in the family's tradition when, as a post-doctoral research fellow, she acted to prevent incorrect data from being used to obtain government funding. Her interference was greatly resented, and she was without a research position for four years. My mother, Elizabeth, had a ready answer for all who expressed concern about what was happening to Margot: "It's no big deal for an O'Toole to throw away a career for a principle." Our parents taught all four of their children to live with integrity and courage. They twinned that foundation with the complementary values of compassion and respect. (Eventually, Margot did prevail. She received several prestigious awards for scientific integrity and went on to a successful career as a research scientist.)

Integrity and courage. Our parents taught all four of their children to stand up for our principles. And they twinned that message with the complementary values of compassion and respect.

Among my father's literary friends was the celebrated, cranky, hard-drinking poet Patrick Kavanagh. Kavanagh fetched up on our doorstep one rainy night, desperate and ill. My mother didn't think twice before taking him in. That rescue stretched into a six-month stay as she nursed him back to health. At the end of his time with us, Kavanagh was writing again and drinking less. He never stopped being difficult. But he grew to love us children. And we loved him back. In 2021, my mother, then 97, published *A Poet in the House: Patrick Kavanagh at Priory Grove*, an acclaimed memoir about those months when Kavanagh was our guest.

Kavanagh was a friend. But my parents' hospitality and compassion extended even to strangers. They welcomed uninvited visitors into our home, including refugees from Hungary and other countries in post-World War II Europe. Then there were the Travelers, nomads who have roamed Ireland for centuries. In the 1950s and '60s, women from the Traveling community would go door-to-door, wrapped in blankets, carrying infants, and invoking Jesus, Mary, and Joseph as they implored householders for whatever could be spared. My mother would greet each woman warmly. They would chat for a while before the Traveler left with milk, food, or spare change, which my mother kept in a bowl near the front door for that purpose. My mother's lesson: every human being deserves our care. That may mean giving them something they need. But it also means listening to them and treating them with dignity.

Those were my foundations, laid more than 60 years in the past and 3,000 miles away from Boston, where I've spent most of my life. At age 75, I am still trying to follow my parents' example.

A Team Sport and a Solo Business

In 1966, when I was 15, my father accepted a teaching job at Boston University. That year, Margot and I moved with him to Massachusetts. The rest of the family arrived the following year. I did well enough in high school to secure a place in Northeastern University's class of 1973, where I largely aced my math courses. But accounting bored me. I paid little attention to it until the final exam approached. Realizing I could flunk the class, I crammed through the night, miraculously crushing the test. I then promptly forgot most of what I'd learned. Years later, I regretted my bad attitude about that course. I should have let Northeastern turn me into a financial genius. It really would have helped when I was trying to build a proper company.

But what distracted me from all my other classes, even the interesting ones, was the Charles River. That meandering waterway, which divides Boston and Cambridge, was (and is) a hugely popular site for rowers. Northeastern's rowing team, which back then rented space from the Riverside Boat Club, was sometimes ranked #1 nationally. During my time there, many of our rowers made the national team, with two competing in the Olympics. It was a culture of discipline, teamwork, and excellence. I had the right physical build for crew: tall and lean, with a strong back from forking hay on my grandfather's farm. I also had the right attitude. I was fully committed to the team and possessed a fierce determination to do nothing less than my personal best.

When I think back on college, that's what I remember most—sun stippling the water; our coach, calling out instructions; before and behind me the straining bodies of my teammates; the healthy aching of my own body. Like many of the rowers, I often trained at the Harvard Stadium, which was just four miles away from Northeastern and on the right (that is to say, the non-Cambridge) side of the Charles. Student athletes would go there with our coaches or on our own and run up and down the steps, a ritual that would later become a touchstone of Gentle Giant's culture. Rowing built my strength and character. The Stadium stairs, meanwhile, helped me maintain a competitive edge. And both activities provided emotional ballast when, in February 1973, my father drowned in a swimming pool.

We had unfinished business, my father and I. While I admired his genius, integrity, and tenacity, as a teenager, I felt he was subjecting me to outsized pressure to succeed. But before he died, I had come to realize that he was only trying to expose me to all the options I had in life. I was looking forward to graduation when he would see how well I had done. I planned to invite him on a bicycle trip around Ireland: something he had once asked of me, and which I had declined. Rowing was what I needed to hold myself together, and where I was always at my best and happiest. Its demands on my concentration provided necessary respite from the desolation I was feeling. When rowing season ended, I ran the Stadium steps five or six times a week to cope with my grief.

After graduating with a degree in engineering from Northeastern, I took a job at the Eaton Corporation, a power-management company on the Fortune 200 list. As part of its management development program, I was moved around the country a lot—four months here, six months there. Some postings were great, others less so. One was horrific. Wanting to return to Boston, I put out feelers and landed a job offer from Polaroid. Before I could decide whether to accept it, other offers started to stream in. I realized I had many options. Among them: not returning to corporate life at all. I decided to take some time and figure out what I genuinely wanted to do.

I banked what savings I had and resolved to live cheaply during this period. I moved in with roommates. I sold my Volvo and bought a car for $10 from a friend—a Peugeot whose floor had completely rusted away. I replaced it with chicken wire covered with fiberglass. That, at least, prevented me from seeing the road passing beneath my feet. I picked up jobs where I could—driving a cab, making deliveries for a freight company, and working occasional night shifts at a cross dock. A few evenings a week I worked at a local convenience store, enjoying the perk of discounted groceries and free about-to-expire meat. A college friend and I took some preliminary steps toward starting a light manufacturing business, but that never gelled.

Then, one night at a party, my roommate's girlfriend asked me to dance.

"Why are you not dancing with Hugh?" I asked her.

"He's really shy," she replied. "I can't persuade him."

"I'll get him out here," I assured her.

"Knock yourself out," she said. "It can't be done."

Hugh was sitting in a chair, chatting. I walked up behind him, reached under his arms, lifted him up, and carried him to the dance floor. There, I started swinging him from side to side. Around us, everyone began to slow-clap. A good sport, Hugh went along with it. After what felt like an eternity but was probably 30 seconds, my arms began to give out. But I had accomplished my mission. Hugh remained where he was and danced the next few numbers.

Like many musicians, Hugh often needed to supplement his income. He'd done some moving jobs that had worked out well for him. Consequently, in the months before the party, he had urged me to give moving a try but had not convinced me to do so. Then, the morning after the dance-floor incident, Hugh resumed his efforts.

"When you picked me up, I didn't feel like a dead body being dragged around," he told me. "It was more like paragliding. It was comfortable.

"You know who you are?" he concluded, triumphantly. "You're the Gentle Giant. That's the name of your moving company!"

"Ha ha, what moving company?" I replied. "I have no interest."

This time, Hugh decided to ignore my resistance. Without telling me, he took out an ad in the *Boston Phoenix*, a weekly alternative newspaper. Under the Moving Services section, the ad read simply "Gentle Giant" and included our phone number. A few days later, the phone rang in our apartment. Hugh answered it.

"It's for you," he said. "Someone wants to hire your moving company."

Taken unawares, I panicked. "I don't even have a truck!" I blurted.

"You can borrow my van," said Hugh.

"What do I charge?"

"How about you charge $13 an hour?" he suggested. "You can give $3 of that to me for the van."

That Saturday morning, I arrived at my first customer's apartment. A dancer, strong and fit, she hefted boxes alongside me, working just as hard as I did. Together, we finished in two hours. I charged her $25. Over the next 32 years, we would move that same customer six more times, as her fortunes rose alongside ours. Little did she know that one day she'd be booking a job with us for $12,500. Little did I know that Gentle Giant would routinely be handling shipments worth a quarter-million dollars.

I had found my life's work. And I didn't know it yet.

My All Was All I Had

I have always been a competitive person, even if the only one I'm competing against is myself. From the beginning, I attacked every moving job as though I were chasing an Olympic medal; racing in and out of a house, bounding up and down stairs. I maintained that insane pace from morning into the night.

The customers were awestruck. Many had survived awful experiences with movers or heard horror stories from their friends about lazy crews, broken dishes, missing boxes, or crushed heirlooms. They would have been happy just to get their belongings from one place to the next in one piece for a fair price. What they got, instead, was this human version of high-speed Tetris, who, true to my "gentle" billing, treated every possession with care. When I was done, they acted like I'd saved their child from drowning. I could have gotten a big ego, I suppose, and believed that I was something special. But to me, it was simple. Someone is paying you by the hour. You're going to give them 100%, for God's sake. How could I not? It never occurred to me to do anything but work as hard as I possibly could for every minute I was paid.

Word about my moving heroics quickly spread. The jobs started to pour in. In those days, I was mostly working on my own, if you can imagine such a thing. Have you ever had a lone mover show up to your house? If so, you likely thought him mad. But I had figured out how to manage even the biggest items on my own. Eventually, I could single-handedly move a grand piano up a staircase. (In case you're wondering—that process involves a specialized moving board, some blocks, and a dolly. Believe it or not, I could even hoist a piano to the upper stories of a home, using a block and tackle and assistance from the customer to hold the rope.) This is the only time in this book that I'll describe a moving technique. Gentle Giant offers numerous training modules that explain how to move things safely and efficiently. But this book is not a how-to manual; it is the story of Gentle Giant.

I did not always work solo. When I was working at the convenience store, I had become friendly with a customer who, it turned out, had his own small moving business. Bruce West and I had an arrangement: if I booked something too big for my van, he'd take the job and let me act as crew chief. And sometimes I would help on his jobs. If he needed me and I was booked, I'd send along a friend I knew met my standards.

Even in these early days as a tiny solo business, I had already formulated the central tenet that is the guiding principle upon which Gentle Giant is built: **a job is not done until the customer is happy**. If customers were difficult, I would take the time to figure out how to resolve the issue and get us on the same page. I would never take the attitude of a lot of service providers, who, when faced with tough customers, put their heads down and push through until they can go home. When a customer asked me for something, I would say yes, so long as it didn't endanger life and limb. That's not the same as believing the customer is always right.

For me, it's about using my brain and strength to solve the customer's issue/problem. Sometimes requests make sense from the get-go, other times it takes effort to understand the customer's perspective. My goal was always clear; I wanted them to be happy. So, even if what they asked was a little silly or would slow things down a bit, I went along with it.

On a job Bruce and I did together, the rain was falling in buckets. We backed his truck right up to the customer's porch and dropped the ramp on the steps. Everything would be wrapped, and we would move quickly. We would only be in the rain for a second or two. It all should have been fine. But the customer was worried that her belongings would get wet. Before we arrived, she had gone out and bought plastic sheeting, a staple gun, and a bunch of 2X4s. She wanted me to build a canopy between the porch and the truck to protect her things. It would mean extra work for zero demonstrable benefit. Clearly, though, she had gone to a lot of trouble. The canopy would give her peace of mind. So, I did as she asked.

Bruce, who had been disassembling furniture inside, came out and saw the structure. "That's the stupidest thing I have seen in my life," he said, without realizing the customer could hear him. As soon as he went back in, I winked at the customer. "He knew you were there," I told her. "That's just his sense of humor."

Bruce wanted to give every customer a perfect move. He did not realize that it sometimes takes more than that to make them happy. At Gentle Giant, we never say "a customer is always right." We know it doesn't matter if they are right or wrong. What is vitally important to us is that we strive to see things from their perspective.

Solo No More

On my very first job, I had discovered something surprising about myself. I loved moving! I loved: the physical challenge and problem-solving, the concrete evidence of achievement, the virtuous exhaustion at the end of a hard day's work, the instant gratification of customers raining down appreciation and gushing about how little they'd expected and how much I'd delivered. What great incentive to deliver even more. I wanted to keep going. But to take on bigger jobs, I would need another pair of hands, another strong back. And it had to be someone who shared my work ethic and enthusiasm for the work. Miraculous as it seems in retrospect, I already knew such a person.

Steven "Rooty" Leonard was a buddy from the Northeastern crew team. From that experience, he understood the drive to push your body as far as it will go, the elation of performing at your peak and seeing the results. And he knew that the most grueling work—making steady progress stroke by stroke or box by box—can become a passion. We immediately became a great team.

Rooty also has a wonderful way with people. He can turn the most annoying situation around with his charming personality. I recall one massive move, which included hauling an entire library—maybe 150 boxes of books—to the attic of the new home in Needham. Rooty and I just about killed ourselves. But we got it done. Then, just as we were settling the bill, the husband turned up and protested that he'd wanted the books in the basement because he needed the attic clear to build the shelving.

The husband and wife were annoyed with one another. I was focused on controlling my own irritation. A good outcome did not seem possible. But as we started shifting the boxes, Rooty cracked jokes and kept things light, drawing the customers in with his banter. The tension soon lifted. The husband even agreed to leave more than half the books in the attic. Against all odds, that job ended on a high note. And I walked away determined to become like Rooty. Always cheerful, always positive, never getting into a funk that made a bad situation worse.

By the summer of 1984, what had begun with an ad my friend, Hugh Norton, placed without even telling me, was consuming my every waking moment. I had always assumed I would one day return to engineering. But I loved working with Rooty. I relished lugging heavy items up and downstairs all day. Most people hate moving so much that they will lie to their best friends to avoid helping them do it. I couldn't imagine doing anything else.

It was time to get serious and build a moving company. I wasn't sure whether my company would be small, like Bruce's, or something more substantial. In my case, it has turned out to be fortuitous that passion vanquished doubt and determination obliterated inexperience. I threw myself into the work that had chosen me. The seeds of what Gentle Giant became were sown in the very beginning. The core values, our company's Giant HEART, spelled out in the Preamble, have been in place since the beginning.

From my family, I learned honesty and respect. Rowing on the Charles brought me the exhilaration and fulfillment of teamwork. My teammates modeled the energy and enthusiasm that I soon would apply to the equally hard, physical labor of moving. As for going above-and-beyond, that's my nature. If you have the power to improve someone's life a little, why wouldn't you do that? If you can improve it a lot, even if it takes a bit longer or costs a few dollars more, isn't that even better?

So, the bones were good. The intentions were right. Now I had only to keep a steady course and build upon my vision.

CHAPTER TWO

Our Mission Defined

Not long after Gentle Giant incorporated, I got a call to move the personal belongings of a business owner from his suburban Boston office to his home. I sent a three-man crew. When our guys got there, however, they discovered that the person who booked the job had made a big mistake. Arrangements should have been made for the relocation of the entire company of 150 employees to a new location in downtown Boston.

"We need some help out here," my crew chief calmly reported.

"What kind of help?" I asked him.

"Well, we need about 25 more movers and three more trucks. Also, 50 dollies and, let's say, 200 file boxes."

It took me a while to realize he was not joking.

That's the moving business—a six-hour job can sometimes turn into a 14- or 16-hour ordeal. That is what I call "a blow-up". It's during a blow-up that a customer can truly come to realize that hiring Gentle Giant was the right choice. The fact is that, from the very beginning of my time as a mover, this has been my commitment: I will, Gentle Giant will, go above-and-beyond to get the job done.

In this particular situation, I would have been more than justified in telling the crew to stick to the original order for service. But to me, it was irrelevant that we were not responsible for the mix-up. We were going to do whatever possible. All our movers were directed to head to that job when their other jobs were finished. At that point in Gentle Giant's history, we had only a few full-time movers. But I maintained a large roster of people who worked for us when their schedules permitted. They all agreed to keep gear stored in their cars. That way, if I needed evening help, they'd be ready to join a job and save the day.

I started calling. By 6 PM, we had a total of 25 movers and four trucks at the site. I enlisted my sister, Jackie, to obtain and deliver the packing materials. She ended up navigating the breakdown lane of Interstate 95 at 20 miles per hour, with boxes piled five feet high, power-strapped to the roof of her Tercel.

By 1 AM the next morning, that company was set up in its new location. Even then, small as we still were, we were demonstrating what's possible when you marshal your resources, approach problems methodically, and don't panic. The pervading ethos of teamwork and camaraderie enabled the Giants to rise to this occasion.

Early Decisions

In October 1983, I flew to Ireland to celebrate my grandfather's 100th birthday. I arrived early, which gave me plenty of time to discuss my new venture with "Dadden," as the family called him. I thought one of the things he told me was especially wise.

"It is the first person you hire and keep around: that person will set the stage for everyone that comes after them. You hold them up to your standard. They must hold the next person to the same standard. And that must follow down through the years."

With his characteristic gift for colorful metaphor, my grandfather laid out the consequences of acting otherwise. "If you hire a person who is not honest or lacks integrity or a great work ethic, that will spread through your company," he said. "Remember, if you piss in your soup, you'll not get it out."

By then, Rooty had already come on board full-time. So, it is my great good fortune that I had already followed my grandfather's counsel.

Rooty, as my first employee, has always been the model of a Gentle Giant. I am so grateful to him for helping me become a better leader and for setting the bar for all who followed after him. He demonstrates what excellence looks like. Forty-four years later, Rooty is Gentle Giant's number-one crane operator. He is also part of the training team.

And when a customer complains, there is no better person than Rooty to calm the waters. He is especially effective when someone claims an item has disappeared during a move. Called out to resolve such situations, Rooty, a devout Catholic, has been known to get down on his knees in front of the customer and pray to St. Anthony for help finding the missing object. Whether or not St. Anthony intervenes, the item invariably shows up. In our business, that's usually because customers, with all they have to pack, think they packed something somewhere, when in fact they packed it somewhere else. For example, when a customer says the milk crate in which they packed their valuables is missing, it is almost always the case that they have forgotten they packed the crate in an as-yet-unpacked box. (Can you imagine how much time we spend looking for things that eventually show up where the customer had forgotten they had been packed?)

When the company consisted of just Rooty and me, I, of course, asked him to become my business partner. I was disappointed when he turned me down. Rooty said he would not feel comfortable in that role. At the time, this made no sense to me. Now, however, I have come to understand how well Rooty understood himself, even way back then when we were both starting out together. The DISC personality tests, which Gentle Giant administered throughout its growth, measure traits such as dominance and influence. Rooty has a tough time being tough. Given the level of execution Gentle Giant demands, our managers must be ready and able to take a tough line with poor performance. Rooty is the patron saint of lost causes. Taking the tough guy stand goes against his nature.

Though he declined my partnership offer, Rooty had very strong views about the type of company I would have to run if I expected him to stick around. I still remember his list of non-negotiables. Chief among them: I must have a clear idea of where I wanted to go and how I intended to get there. In other words, what did I think the future of Gentle Giant looked like? One thing I was sure of was that we would continue to provide great service. I knew I could ensure that so long as the service was provided exclusively by Rooty, myself and some former teammates. But how would we maintain these high standards if Gentle Giant were to scale up?

I'd gotten an earful from customers about their miserable experiences with other movers. Now I needed to understand what made those businesses so awful. What kinds of cut corners, dubious behaviors, and misaligned incentives were giving the industry such a bad name? Call it the "study of worst practices." And, of course, I also needed to learn the more conventional best practices, with the ultimate goal of surpassing them.

I began with observation. Back then, I rode my bicycle everywhere, and this made it easier to stop and observe whenever I saw a moving crew. I would take a seat across the street, pull out a book, and just watch them. Often, what I'd see was the crew chief—usually a slightly older guy—camped out in the back of the truck, smoking a cigarette, and yelling orders. "Oh my God! What are you doing? Jesus don't put that there! Use your fucking head!"

Of course, I saw hard-working people, too. But the pervasiveness of disrespect and laziness was dismaying. Curious about the owners who were sending out such crews, I decided to pay them visits. To a man, they were all gracious and welcoming. They were more than willing to share their stories and divulge their helpful hints. When discussing other challenges faced in this low-margin, labor-intensive industry, owners were frank. "I don't mind sharing all my secrets with you. My hat is off to anyone who can make it in this business," said a company owner who became an early advisor and—until the day he died—a dear friend.

There was one owner, Jim Clark, whose crews had impressed me. He seemed to be able to retain good workers. Jim held his movers to very strict standards. For example, the crews used rubber bands to keep pads on furniture. At the end of a job, Jim would weigh the bands and dock the crew's bonus money if any were missing. I considered running that tight a ship, but while I admired Jim's high standards, I feared these practices would dampen morale. I decided to foster a culture of trust instead.

When I asked these owners what their biggest challenge was, the answer always was: "finding good help." As I listened to them, the root of most of their problems became clear. They had not benefited from following my grandfather's advice. They had allowed people who lacked a strong work ethic and/or strong personal values to join their workforce. Often, the problem had begun with a well-meaning favor—the hiring of a relative or friend. The wrong people were often being retained out of loyalty or inertia.

Moving is a seasonal business, and most of the hiring happens in April and May. These owners prioritized hiring based on experience and were relieved when they filled their roster. Meanwhile, every mover who has been fired for any of a myriad reasons knows that during this surge, the owners are desperate for experienced movers. To my amazement, some owners told me that it was so hard to find experienced people that they had, on occasion, re-hired people they themselves had previously fired. The rationalization for these rehires was usually, "I hoped he had learned his lesson." And when they hired experienced people they did not know, they often did not even check references—shrugging and saying things like, "How else am I going to find someone with experience?"

As a result, they were saddled with bad actors such as slackers, bullies and phonies. Bad actors bring down companies as they eat up managers' time, who struggle with the chaos (unreliability to substance abuse) they create. With this focus on finding people they did not have to train, they randomly mixed the bad with the good. The consequences of that are wide and deep. Good workers flee toxic environments. I also heard endless whining from many of the owners about customers. They shared horror stories about people dragging them into small-claims court over cooked-up damage reports. Others described being forced to file lawsuits for non-payment. Virtually all had anecdotes about getting snookered or screwed over. They talked about the customers as if they were the enemy.

Listening to all this cemented in my mind that I would never get into conflicts with customers. I resolved to develop the negotiating skills to find common ground when customers made unreasonable demands. Being able to see things from the customers' perspective has become a core practice at Gentle Giant.

Policies and a Partner

Talking to these owners helped me define the tenets of the business I envisioned:

- We would seek out the best people and pay them as generously as we could.
- We would make sure new hires meet our standards and not delay letting them know if they were not a fit.
- Our salespeople would make good salaries. They would not be on commission. This would eliminate any temptation to "spin" when trying to clinch a deal and would promote full disclosures to our customers. It would also maximize teamwork within the sales department.

- Our movers would be employees with full benefits—no contractors or workers from a labor pool.
- We would nurture relationships with honorable real estate agents and would not give kickbacks for referrals.
- We would hire and train our own people—not poach from other companies.
- We would create an environment free from slackers and whiners.

With these tenets in place, I turned my attention to the actual business aspects of running a business. I had enough self-awareness to realize I was not the best person to oversee an organizational infrastructure for a growing company. As someone who was bored by college accounting courses, I clearly should not appoint myself to be in charge of the financial side of things. It's true that, up until that point, I had been handling the financial records, but my methods could best be described as "by the seat of my pants." Payroll is a good example. I would say to a mover, "I'll see you in the yard on Saturday. Would you bring a list of all the jobs you've worked on and how much I owe you?" Then I'd write that into my ledger. This improvisational style of financial management did not fit scale-up ambitions. I needed to find a professional financial manager.

To my great good fortune, the solution was staring me in the face. By that time, Rooty had recruited a good friend of his, Doug Deitz, a world-class rower. He needed a job to tide him over until the right opportunity in his field emerged. I had worked on the trucks with Doug for many months. He was a phenomenal mover. I set his schedule to accommodate his job interviews, and fortunately for us, he kept holding out for the right opportunity in Boston.

Doug had the Gentle Giant HEART. I knew his mettle. I trusted him completely. **And** he had recently finished an MBA at Boston University.

He had a methodical, operations mentality. He was a person of unshakable integrity. When he talked about the kind of company he wanted to join, it seemed to me he was describing the company I dreamt of building.

In August 1984, I asked Doug to be my business partner. He accepted. We agreed to capitalize the company at $10,000 in a 70/30 split. Doug and I were the perfect team. Years later, when I began talking to consultants, they challenged my decision to make Doug my partner. "Why did you give this guy 30% when you could have just hired someone?" they asked. But that wouldn't have worked for me. I wanted someone with skin in the game and the same passion and commitment as I had. He was organized and detail oriented, and I was the entrepreneur. Hallelujah! We were on our way.

Doug quickly and methodically began putting the processes in place that would turn Gentle Giant into a well-oiled operation primed for growth. Before he came on board, I had kept things dead simple. For example, to avoid ever owing money, I paid for everything upfront. When Doug took over the books, it finally felt safe to allow ourselves to be billed. In the ensuing 41 years, Gentle Giant has never made a late payment.

We had been renting our trucks, but a serious moving company should have its own trucks. Research pointed me toward a $39,000 Iveco. I tried to get a loan. But every bank turned me down, despite a $15,000 down-payment and a well-established revenue stream. It was not easy for me, a 6-foot-6, 33-year-old who has been out of the house for more than a decade, to ask my mom, a widowed public-school teacher, for help. She did not have the money, but not for a second did she falter. She re-mortgaged her house. A beautiful 24-foot truck was delivered by Christmas. On January 2, 1985, we incorporated the business.

We were so busy that we didn't even have time to design uniforms or put a logo on the truck. More than a year passed before we addressed these issues. Most moving company trucks display the business name in generic block letters. I wanted something more distinctive. Robert Swift, one of our legendary movers, is also a talented artist. Robert designed our lettering so that the lower-case "g" of "gentle" appears to sprout like a bud from the bar on the upper-case "G" of Giant. Robert's elegant and clever lettering has served us well all these years. (He recently retired, having run jobs until he was 71 years old.)

We have kept that distinctive lettering logo and added a pair of giant feet on either side. (This modification was designed by Carol Lasky and her team at Cahoots Design.) Soon after this, the Giants began wearing uniforms—tee shirts bearing our logo. Purple, gold, and green became our colors. With the logos splashed on our trucks, and a steadily increasing number of Gentle Giant vehicles on the road, we drew attention all around Boston. The way our customers' children reacted to the arrival of the Giants was especially gratifying. To them, it was as though creatures out of fairytales were pulling into their driveways.

The Big Idea Takes Form

As far as I was concerned, I had my business plan: Hire only great people. And this plan worked. As Doug and I began building a full-time staff, we brought onboard intrinsically motivated people. Didn't need the carrot—didn't need the stick. The kind of employees who show up every morning, determined to give value for money, who work hard for the sheer satisfaction they get from doing their best. In the next chapter, I'll explain in detail how we've maintained the high quality of our hires. For now, suffice it to say that every new Giant sets out to prove to the customer that, by hiring us, they made a great decision. As a team, we attack each job with gleeful enthusiasm and meet each challenge with unwavering determination. Every job, through referrals, leads to many others.

It often happens that, as a business takes off, entrepreneurs of service companies transition from the front line, customer-facing work to the relative sequestration of oversight work from an office. With Doug's hand in firm control, I was still able to spend much of my time on the trucks. My love of being on the trucks—working with the crews and interacting with the customers—has never waned. And on the truck is where I felt I could best serve my company—both as a model and coach to employees and as the company's face to customers. I also loved lining up the movers and making sure we had all the equipment we would need to make each day a success.

As Gentle Giant's business quickly grew, so did our need for trucks. For a while, it made financial sense to rent additional ones. On a typical day, I was up at 6:15 AM and on my bike, arriving at UHAUL by 6:45 AM. When the business opened at 7 AM, I would be at the head of the line. I would rent a truck, outfit it back at our base, and give the crew the paperwork. Then, I would bike back to UHAUL, grab another truck, outfit that one, and hightail it to a customer's house, where another mover would be waiting for me. At day's end, I'd return the truck and then head back home to face the answering machine.

That answering machine would be full of messages from customers eager to book us. It was an intense and exhausting period. My outgoing message said, "I'm away on a moving job and might not get back until late. Please let me know what time you go to bed so I can avoid disturbing you". If the potential customer didn't go to bed until 1 AM, he would probably get a call at 12:45, and that would be fine with him. He'd say, "My friend told me I'd be crazy to call anyone else. Can I book a move?"

There were long stretches where I was working seven days a week and averaging thirteen-hour days. I was fine with this; it was what I signed up for. On Labor Day 1984, when Doug agreed to be my partner, I made a resolution. I would work this hard for two years, and if I could not afford to hire the staff that I would need to get back to a normal life, I would call it quits.

For the first few years, Gentle Giant operated out of my apartment. We outgrew that and took over two rooms in an artist's studio. We leased a parking space from MIT for our trucks and a storage trailer. By then, we had begun hiring at a fast pace. In 1989, we leased our first warehouse and, during the August rush, employed 92 full- and part-time people. True to our founding principles, they were all our own staff—no contractors.

In these very early days, I kept a growing list of men who loved working on the trucks part-time. Most of these movers were athletes who were either students or working in another field. My system for booking jobs was simple. When a call came in, if I was available myself, if I could, I would book the job. I would make calls until I found someone who was available to work with me. If I found a second person, I would be available for another booking in that time slot. I would repeat this process if other bookings came in.

The beauty of this system was twofold. First, there were people on my list who relished the opportunity to be matched to jobs as I booked them. Secondly, since I would be the crew chief on the last job booked, even if my list of vetted movers were depleted and I had to rely on an inexperienced person in my own crew, I could be certain the customer would have a great moving experience.

And here is proof that a values-driven workplace culture spurs success: the camaraderie, pay, loyalty, and work satisfaction of working for Gentle Giant were such that this system worked seamlessly. When, as happened in the move described in the opening of this chapter, I needed people at a moment's notice, they showed up. I never fail to show appreciation for such loyalty, and my policy is to always be as generous as possible with the movers.

Occasionally, I would get a call from a price shopper. Those types of conversations typically open with a Bostonian voice asking,

"Whada ya chaahge?"

"I will tell you what we charge," I would say. "But first, there are some more important questions you need answered."

My job was to establish a friendly connection with these customers. It was wonderful when someone who'd been calling around looking for the lowest price would say, "OK. I'd like to book with you."

After one particularly exhausting day, my sister Jackie dropped by with some takeout.

"I guess this is the only way we can get to see you," she said, as I cut things short to get to my callbacks. Seeing my list, she said, "This is ridiculous. Why don't you go to bed and let me handle this?"

"No, thanks. It will take all night to explain all this to you."

"Oh, really?" she said.

Jackie ended up quitting her job and put an end to my late nights. She recently retired after 40 years as a top salesperson.

At first, Doug and I took a strict "company revenue first" approach to our personal compensation. We were each paid $13.50/hour, but only for the hours we were working on the trucks (i.e., generating revenue). About a year after he became my partner, Doug figured it was safe to put us both on a modest salary. Two years in, I had reached my goal.

I was now positioned to hire people and allow myself a more normal life—no more 16-hour days.

At that juncture, with Gentle Giant having reached steady growth and financial stability, I could have changed the way I vetted new candidates. Instead, I made what I consider to be my crucial foundational decision. My interview process would remain a "Day On The Truck With Me." My business plan was "Hire Only Great People," and during this start-up phase, I stuck with this foolproof selection process. After one job together, I could usually determine whether I could confidently schedule a candidate to work with one of our crew chiefs. If not, then he and I would have a friendly conversation. If I enjoyed working with him, I'd say so, and if I thought he was not cut out for the job, I'd tell him. A handful of times, a candidate didn't make it to the end of the job. In those instances, I would call him a cab or point out the subway station and finish the job by myself.

Of course, later, when we were growing faster than could be accommodated by the "Day On The Truck With Me" interview process, we devised other methods that ensured we continued (and still ensure we continue) to adhere to our original plan of hiring only great people. The direct result is that we have raised the standard for what people expect of movers. Now, many good companies are trying to emulate our model. If we hire and train someone who doesn't meet our standards and we let them go, they are typically snapped up by another company that knows the value of our training.

As we grew rapidly, our infrastructure needs, of course, expanded rapidly as well. Over the next few years, we added equipment, trucks, and state-of-the-art warehouses. This crucial part of the business was not where my heart lay, and it ate up much of my time. It dawned on me that we already had an employee who was the perfect person to oversee these essential parts of running a moving company. John Pacocha, known to all at Gentle Giant as J.P., came to us as a mover in

1985. Another Division 1 rower, J.P. has an engineering degree from Northeastern, which could have been his ticket anywhere. In fact, at one point, another Giant, who was leaving to start what would become a successful company, invited J.P. to become his partner. J.P. loved our culture and opted to stay. Appreciative of his loyalty and impressed by his work ethic and technical knowledge, Doug and I brought him on as a 10% partner in 1990. For 35 years he has been instrumental in our success and is now a VP.

Larry and J.P. in the early days moving the Boston Chinatown Lions

Our Mission: Changing Public Perception

At the time I decided to start a moving company, it was clear to me that the public in general regarded moving as a service that could be bought off the shelf, like a standardized, pre-packaged commodity. Everyone understands that you get more when you pay more for a quality hotel or a well-regarded attorney. In my industry, however, the mindset was that, regardless of the price, moving was inevitably a horrible experience, so why not grit your teeth and get through it as cheaply as possible? Gentle Giant's mission was big—we had to change how people perceived the moving industry. The quality of the service we provided would be so extraordinarily high that people would look back on the move experience with pleasure and appreciation.

I knew at this point that the only way to fulfill this mission was to hire and retain great people (and I had figured out how to do that) and compensate them well. All a moving company has is execution. We were going to be the company for those willing to pay for an enjoyable experience—one that also ensured all precious belongings were safely moved. As such, we weren't particularly focused on price. The idea was to build our reputation, while our customers raved to their friends, and prices could rise over time. My conviction that the quality of our movers would allow us to soar above the competition continues to be reinforced with each new appreciative customer.

In 1991, we debuted at #395 on the Inc. 500: *Inc. Magazine*'s ranking of America's fastest-growing private companies. The Inc. 500 (now the Inc. 5000) ranks companies by sales growth. I basked then, as I still do, in this achievement. Most of the companies on the list back then—and most on the list today—had national, sometimes global, footprints and significant marketing budgets. The largest sectors represented included tech, financial services, advertising, and media.

I wonder whether any Inc. 500 company other than Gentle Giant achieved its growth entirely through word-of-mouth. In the five years between our incorporation and 1990 (the year covered by the 1991 ranking) we grew to $2.3 million in revenue. Virtually all that business came to us through referrals. Review sites didn't exist back then, of course. We did no marketing and very little advertising. For instance, we bought ads in a couple of free local LGB publications. Those were inexpensive and very effective. Readers who saw them greatly appreciated our support for their community.

Our business grew because people were telling others about the fabulous experience they had with the Giants. Customers reported that others didn't just recommend us; their friends browbeat them into agreeing to give us a try. One customer told me that his sister threatened to never speak to him again if he didn't hire the Giants. Another guy said he hired us because we had been praised to the skies by some of the most annoying people at his workplace. He claimed that he actually looked forward to a bad experience so he could contradict them. But he ended up having to agree that we were pretty damn good. And he became a customer for life.

Play It Safe or Shoot for the Stars?

A few years after making the Inc. 500, I found myself at a crossroads. Every day, more movers head out on more trucks to serve more customers. As sales rose rapidly, we were poised to graduate from the status of small business to mid-sized company. If we committed to it, I believed we would have almost unlimited prospects. I was in love with Gentle Giant. It had become a huge part of my identity. Of course, I envisioned an amazing future for it. I felt wonderful about what we had accomplished and was "all-in" for accomplishment on a larger scale.

Still, I was running around like a crazy person, trying to keep standards high. "Don't make the mistake everyone makes," people warned me. "You're going to lose control of your business. Create a big overhead. Compromise on quality. Collapse in flames."

I was getting advice to sell and invest the proceeds in a new startup. There was some logic to that course. I understood that launching a business and growing one are very different challenges. I had proven to be a successful startup entrepreneur. Whether I could manage a large company was another matter entirely.

The alternative was to ease up on growth, reach a manageable level and then throttle back. "Stay small; keep it all," as one friend (repeatedly) put it. Doug saw the merits of that argument. "We have a good thing going here", he said. "We're stable and profitable." Significant growth would require us to build a big, expensive infrastructure, which would be challenging to maintain in an industry as seasonal as moving.

As Doug described it, we risked becoming "an elephant on roller skates, vulnerable to every fluctuation in the market." Doug is a candid guy. Still, he tried to be diplomatic when arguing that, if we expanded, my seat-of-the-pants management style would likely drive us into a ditch.

I was on the horns of a dilemma. The issue was not whether we should grow the company. The company was growing almost exponentially due to our repeat and referral business. But a decision had to be made: Do we devise a business strategy to keep us in the three-to-five-million-dollar range over the long term, or do we allow growth to continue unabated? The former strategy presented very little risk. We could raise our prices, keep our infrastructure costs stable, and increase our margins. The latter strategy presented great challenges and opportunities—and would involve great risk. The opportunity was the potential to grow into a larger, more valuable company with expanded career opportunities for employees.

According to conventional wisdom and basically everybody whose advice I sought, the biggest challenge would be maintaining quality in the face of rapid expansion. Being told it couldn't be done in the moving business fueled my competitiveness. I yearned to prove the naysayers wrong. I was hungry to demonstrate that we could sustain quality and keep winning in the marketplace.

We kept growing.

CHAPTER THREE

Finding and Keeping Giants with HEART

I haven't met many people as eager to prove themselves as James O'Donovan. Throughout the hiring process, he kept insisting he could outwork anyone. Still, I questioned his physical ability to do the job. An experienced Giant had not recommended him. He touted his work in construction, but would he hustle all day while carrying heavy objects? Well, I would find out. The next day, I scheduled him to work with me. I chose a tough job that could have used a third mover. I knew we were in for a long day. Faced with a physical challenge, would he dig in harder? Or would he start to fade?

We set up a box chain. James would bring out a box, carry it halfway to the truck, and hand it to me. While I was loading it, he would head back toward the house for another box. At one point, I decided to whip past him to get the next box. I did this to gauge his reaction. He was either going to be the type of person who would not let this happen again, or it wouldn't bother him. This technique has helped identify people who take pride in meeting a standard. James, as it turned out, was a person of that first type. He was not going to let anybody out hustle him. He kept pace with me as I raced in and out of the house. He hefted two book boxes at a time. As we hauled heavy items down the stairs, he was vigilant about keeping them away from the walls. He had the grit and pride we look for in our Giants.

He never complained, but as we began unloading, I could see the juice drain out of him. I tried to lighten his load by using a piano board to get the heavier items up the stairs. Toward the end, as we attacked a mountain of book boxes, he finally ground to a halt. "Don't worry," I told him. "Just fold these pads. I'll run in the last boxes."

On the drive home, close to midnight, James was silent. At last, he spoke.

"I disgraced myself today," he said. "You don't have to pay me."

"Don't be ridiculous," I replied. "Of course, I'll pay you."

"I don't deserve it," James said. "If this was an exam, I'd have flunked it."

"You didn't flunk," I told him. "Maybe you were just a D. But I saw the effort you put in today. If you keep putting in that kind of effort, you'll soon be an A+."

What I saw in James wasn't just a hard worker—although he was that. I also saw someone who acknowledged his own weaknesses and wanted to get better. Someone with the patience to improve steadily. Most importantly, I saw a person who was open to honest feedback and to coaching. And sure enough, James became an A+ mover and worked for Gentle Giant for many years.

Testing for The Right Mindset

Harvard Stadium, the country's oldest, comprises 31 levels of concrete seats, divided into 37 sections arranged in a horseshoe. For more than 120 years, college and professional athletes, Olympians and fitness enthusiasts alike have scaled and descended its grand total of 3,441 steps. Every step you climb is 15 inches high. People who are top class athletes will run every section. But for the average person, it's more of a series of deep, uphill lunges (which is a great workout).

If you stand at the bottom of the first section, gazing up at concrete gray rise upon concrete gray rise, you will feel both intimidated and inspired. As your eyes pan slowly across the sections, you will see stadium runners rendered tiny by distance within the huge stadium. Your legs and lungs will likely start asking you if you really want to do this, but a resolute brain will reply "yes" with the first leap up on a concrete rise.

The Harvard Stadium steps played an important role in my college days, both physically and—after my father's death—emotionally. Many of the world-class athletes who joined me in the early days of Gentle Giant had trained there regularly. From the beginning to the present, the Harvard Stadium steps have helped us identify people who are a good fit for our HEART culture.

Every week—sometimes twice a week—we convene at the Stadium with a group of fresh hires. Then, up we go. In May, as many as 20 movers may start on the same day. A handful of current employees also participate. We start at 6:30 AM, when the pillars at the top are bathed in shadow, making the ascent seem like the approach to an ancient temple. Most of our runners will wear company tank tops and T-shirts, peeling them off as their body heat rises and their clothes soak through.

I regularly run alongside the new hires, every step of the way, and members of our leadership team and training department also join regularly. Our participation is important. It shows that we lead by example. It lets those joining the company know that we are teammates—united in our commitment to staying fit and giving "above-and-beyond" service to our customers. Our participation is also important from another perspective. Side by side, together we pit will and stamina against a daunting obstacle. This is a powerful bonding ritual that sets the tone for a relationship defined by mutual respect and support.

Performance at the Stadium, it turns out, is a pretty good predictor of performance on the job. People who attack the steps with determination and grit will—in the end—ride high with the pride of personal and team achievement. They will make wonderful Gentle Giant movers. They are people who won't quit. They won't whine or complain. When it feels as though they've reached the end of their strength and resources, they will dig deeper. Those are the people I want to represent Gentle Giant in front of our customers. Those are the people I want to work with every day. And perhaps, most importantly, those people will know they are joining a company that expects and values the kind of effort their own self-respect demands, and they will be working with like-minded people.

An in-shape athlete can run the whole stadium in less than half an hour. A top Division 1 athlete can clock in under 21 minutes. In an ideal world, all candidates would finish within 40 minutes. We certainly do not reject people who are slower than that, even much slower. It is true that we are assessing physical fitness. Much more importantly, we are assessing intensity of the effort expended. Grit and determination are prerequisites.

When you see determination, you are looking at potential. Even a candidate who is not in the best physical condition can quickly get in shape on the job. When a new mover makes a best effort, regrets not performing as well as hoped, and asks for a chance to come back and try again, that's a sign that we have made a good hire. People like that will keep returning to the Stadium on their own initiative, running circuits until they make the grade.

When you get down to it, that's what you need to know in order to hire the very best candidates—not where they went to school or what jobs they've done or whether they've got a binder full of references. You need to know whether they want to be in an environment where above-and-beyond is routine, and they need to know what we mean by "above-and-beyond."

If someone doesn't have the right attitude or mental stamina that Gentle Giant requires, then that, too, becomes apparent. The steps don't lie. Every year, a handful will be gone by the time the rest of us have completed our circuit. They'll make it through a few sections, then head out, often muttering some version of, "I don't need this crap."

Isn't that wonderful? Music to my ears! I am so grateful when the Stadium helps people decide whether this job is right for them. The company can hire with confidence, the candidates can "self-sort," and best of all, no customer gets sent a mover without a Giant HEART. That's one way we manage to find great hires.

Knowing What to Look For

Although the Harvard Stadium experience has helped Gentle Giant test for a particular type of grit we need, some other approach is likely to be more suitable for many other start-up entrepreneurs. What is of paramount importance is having a clear idea of the characteristics you are looking for and an understanding of why they are needed. Figuring out how to find, hire, and train people with these characteristics is the first part of the process. Providing an environment that will support and retain them is the next, and more important, challenge.

From the beginning, I realized I would need to find employees who would be:

- Honest, ethical, and respectful
- Passionate about serving others and attentive to detail
- Empathetic, good communicators with a talent for making connections and building trust
- Optimistic and good humored
- Collaborative problem solvers
- Hard working and eager to test personal limits

- Great teammates invested in helping others to develop
- Even-tempered and unflappable
- Unfazed under pressure
- Willing and able to call out a colleague's bad behavior in ways that are both supportive and empathetic.

My vision of Gentle Giant as a big company was predicated on a sustained ability to identify, recruit and retain people who would embrace our HEART values. It was clearly a search that considered only those with an already established record of superior performance and selfless teamwork could not sustain growth. Simply put, identifying great candidates when you need 10 employees is easier than when you need 100 or 1000. I realized that we needed to identify candidates who had not yet proven themselves as superior performers and selfless teammates, but who had the potential to do so.

I refer to top tier candidates as "Should-do-the-Job" (SDTJ) people. These are people who, by their very nature, will give their very best, and only their very best, whatever the task. That is because they are incapable of accepting anything less from themselves. For me, an important and reliable indicator of having found an SDTJ person is someone who takes obvious, unflagging enjoyment in doing their very best. They approach their work, whatever it is, with the attitude that the work is worthy of their best effort. I look for enthusiasm, good humor and commitment to excellence. People with these qualities create a thriving, high-morale workplace for their co-workers. The customers reap great benefits. I estimate that such SDTJ people constitute about 10-20% of a candidate pool.

SDTJ people are notable for their determination, optimism, and integrity. Call it character, although that's not a word you hear much in the talent-assessment trade. Character can be tough to judge from a resume or an interview. But it shows up early on the job, especially in a service industry where your people are your product—where every moment they're in front of a customer is an opportunity to elevate or lower your company's reputation. Not surprisingly, because such top performers are relatively rare, they are in very high demand.

There is another type of candidate that constitutes approximately 20 to 30 per cent of the workforce. We see them as AAAC—Avoid at All Costs. Their goal, it seems, is to get away with doing as little as possible. Beware, they might also be experts at navigating job interviews. In my view, it is very important to avoid getting saddled with people who intend to put in just enough effort to avoid getting fired. Luckily, we have the Stadium to protect us from this, but if you make the unfortunate mistake of hiring such people, they will reveal their true attitudes soon after being hired. You need to have processes in place that allow a gentle easing out the door. Otherwise, as my grandfather warned, they will start to drag down the company work ethic.

Around 50-70% of candidates fall somewhere between the first two groups. For them, the primary goal is to fit in, be accepted, and secure a position. If they find themselves in a negative culture where people are whining and complaining, they can, without even realizing it, be pulled into it. Among these, however, are people who, when surrounded by positive energy and a culture of excellence, are genuinely thrilled to be part of it. They will forge identities fully integrated with the values around them. And this is the secret of Gentle Giant's success: we have built a culture, a Giant HEART culture, within which people who did not necessarily join us as SDTJ people become SDTJ people.

Developing skills can be challenging—or not—depending on the employee. Improving character is much harder and more complex. The former requires an employee to become a better mover. The latter requires him to become a better person. My solution: the solution I recommend to any entrepreneur is to provide in-house coaching aimed at developing those with the potential to be SDTJ people to become SDTJ people. My firm belief, buttressed by my extensive observation, personal experience, and success by all objective standards, is that this is the only path to scale up while sustaining workforce quality.

So, the challenge is: how do you find and develop those with SDTJ potential among those candidates in that middle group that do not present as SDTJ people on Day 1? Since our pivot to becoming a larger company, our hiring goals have remained the same. We hire and retain as many top-tier candidates as we can. Among the next tier of candidates (the majority), we rely on a selection and probationary process that reliably identifies those with development potential. Once hired, if employees do not demonstrate the right attitude or aptitude, a friendly conversation can ease them out the door. We rely on these processes to protect us from anyone whose work ethic and/or attitude is incompatible with our commitment to excellent service to our customers.

It's fine to start with a "profile" of the person you are seeking. Some employers like to hire veterans, who they believe excel at executing when directed and can adapt in stressful situations. (Gentle Giant also values those qualities.) Some prefer candidates who have held leadership positions in their schools, churches, or communities. Those who prioritize creativity may want folks who have started a business or invented something. But if your candidate search criteria are focused narrowly on who the person is, you will be walking away from enormous human potential. In my view, the key to success is learning how to recognize those who, under the appropriate conditions, will become stalwart supporters of a culture of excellence. Great employees are those who embody the values of the company's leadership.

The Strenuous Ups and Downs of The Gentle Giant Probationary Period

Our hiring process is the cornerstone of our success. We have an intense 90-day probationary period (described in detail below) during which candidates are closely observed and evaluated by veteran movers. Our criteria are clear and transparent, and we give people opportunities (often repeated opportunities) to raise their performance to our required levels. We are evaluating determination, enthusiasm, teamwork, responsiveness to feedback, consistently respectful attitudes, the ability to make empathetic connections with others, and, above all else, forthrightness and honesty. This process does require a significant investment of time—and that time is very well spent.

The process is such that, most often, it is the candidates themselves who decide that Gentle Giant is not a fit for them. People who are looking for a job that requires minimal effort do not make it through the first two days. Our experienced evaluators and trainers are on the alert for people who fall short of the Giant HEART. (In fact, our trainers evaluate based on each of the HEART values.) At the end of our probationary period, we have great confidence in the people we are sending out on the trucks.

I believe that probationary periods—where the fit between the candidate and the company's values and goals can be objectively and transparently assessed—are key to entrepreneurial success. I have spoken with many business leaders seeking advice on how to address employees whose behavior creates a toxic work environment. I am left wondering how such people managed to survive the probationary period. I conclude that the probationary process was not adequately designed or followed. With the Gentle Giant probationary period, it is extremely rare to reach the end without the decision being obvious.

Veteran Assessments and Self-Assessments

We often use video interviews for a first screen of applicants. But all those we hire, we will have spoken to in person. When interviewing candidates, our recruiters and HR people listen very closely to responses and pay attention to facial expressions and body language. They are extremely sensitive to even the smallest signs of defensiveness, arrogance, unreliability, or cavalier attitude. Here's why that matters so much. If I asked you to name professions for which trust is paramount, you'd probably mention day-care providers and grade-school teachers, pilots, doctors, nurses, and police. Movers might not occur to you. But consider this: these are people who come into your home, handle your most precious possessions, and do their work in proximity to your children and pets. We cannot ask for our customers' trust if we cannot trust each other. Honesty always comes first—as it does in our HEART values.

We also administer self-assessment tests to candidates intended to elicit how they measure up—from Below Average to Exceptional—on a dozen traits we consider critical for the job. Those traits range from our Giant HEART values to things like stamina, common sense, and concern for quality. People who think they excel at everything probably lack self-awareness. Good luck coaching them. They have yet to accept the need to learn new skills and willingness to listen. Many candidates start out on those assessments claiming across-the-board excellence, presumably for fear that admitting a weakness will hurt their chances of getting hired. At age 19, they say they've got everything figured out. When that happens, we use it as a life lesson right out of the gate: an opportunity to discuss how much we value transparency and self-awareness. Usually, that elicits more realistic answers and launches some revealing conversations. ("Why did you change your tolerance-for-the-unexpected rating to Below Average?") If, on another pass, a candidate still describes himself as the Second Coming, then that is, indeed, a big red flag. Very critical to the probationary process is that, during this time, all our candidates work on the trucks with experienced crew chiefs. We believe you learn more about a person while working with them than you do sitting behind a desk during an interview. We rely heavily on the assessments by our crew chiefs.

The Meaning of Gentle-Giant-Nice

Throughout the process of identifying and vetting employees, we naturally want to make sure that they are nice people. Usually, that's not difficult. A person with a passion for service and helpfulness is highly likely to also be "nice." We are looking for that proactive, service-oriented version of nice. I want people who are sensitive to those around them. People who notice someone in need and say: "What can I do to help!"

Here is the kind of thing that happens when you hire people who are proactively nice. There was a woman whose car had broken down in the travel lane of a highway. She was terrified. Cars were zooming past her on both sides. In the rear-view mirror, she could see them swerving to avoid her. Surely, she would be hit!

Then another vehicle slowed and, with flashers on, came to a stop behind her. It was a Gentle Giant truck. One of the movers climbed down, set up hazard triangles and began waving traffic to the left. The other two pushed her to safety in the breakdown lane. Later, she called and told me that story. I was happy to hear it but not surprised. That's what actively nice people do. That's what we look for when we hire.

One of the most famous stories of Giant lore tells of how the innate kindness of one of our movers got us into trouble—trouble that led to a very different kind of phone call. On a cold winter's day in the mid-'80s, Theirry Louvet, a powerful mover who had rowed for France in the Olympics, was transporting a couple of enormous wooden crates that had been used in an international job. He was driving back to our base on the MIT campus. The university had been generous in its terms for leasing us space there. He spotted a bunch of people camping out in a vacant lot. They were protesting the university's plans to develop housing that did not include affordable units.

The protestors had a fire going in an oil drum and as Theirry reported, "looked ready to freeze to death". Not realizing that it was MIT property, he stopped, hefted the crates over the fence and lugged them into the lot so they could be used for shelter. The protestors were extremely grateful. But the next day, my main contact at MIT called me, so irate that he was barking like a dog. How dare we aid and abet people protesting against MIT? I apologized profusely and Rooty went there and negotiated (for a fee) the return of the crates.

I want every Gentle Giant to have the same generous instincts as Theirry. If, as happened in this case, unforeseen conflicts arise because of such kindness, we are ready to meet the challenge of finding mutually acceptable resolutions. In fact, this is a good example of how my determination to find a mutually acceptable solution has been put to the test.

Recruiting

Roughly 70% of new hires come to us through referrals, which is a tremendous boon. (Just 4% of companies with referral programs successfully hire even 30% of employees that way, according to the career site Zippia.) It's hard to go wrong if you design the kind of business that employees present to their friends almost as a gift. And not just friends. We've had dozens of workers whose parents were Gentle Giants 25 or 30 years ago.

Referrals are very important in our business, but we do not pay for them. That is a policy that others in the company have pushed back against over the years. But I have several reasons for sticking with it. For example, more than one employee may recommend the same person. Or resentment can fester if a recommended person isn't hired. My principal aversion to referral fees, however, is more fundamental. If employees need financial incentives to encourage friends to join your business, then you are doing something wrong. You shouldn't have to bribe them.

We also use recruiters. All are on staff because we've found that outsourcing that function produces poor candidates. Demand for workers is seasonal, which means recruiting isn't anyone's full-time job. In less busy months, our recruiters also work in other functions, such as sales, quality control, or on the trucks. Virtually all have been movers at one time or another. Consequently, they know what the job requires and can make a pretty good guess on whether candidates have the right stuff.

We take extra care when evaluating candidates with prior moving experience. Of course, given our commitment to an in-house probationary period for anyone who represents us to our customers, we never, ever, draw on labor pools. (I have heard terrible reports about jobs done with workers from labor pools.) We are very cautious when hiring experienced professionals from other companies. We don't want people who have learned the wrong lessons to lower our standards. However, every so often, an experienced true professional moving expert has come through our door. That is rare, but what a joy when it does happen, as it did with Chuck Re. We were lucky that Chuck chose to spend a six-month gap in his career with us. He was a perfect fit for our culture, and he shared his expertise in the finer points of handling and loading valuable items. He had dropped out of high school to work for his uncle's moving business. His commitment to excellence was extraordinary. I will never forget our interview, during which he helped me move an 800-pound piano into our warehouse.

Like most moving companies, we do peak business in the warm months, when volume doubles or triples. Aligning the moving season with school vacations is a huge boon for companies like ours. Many of our seasonal workers are still in college. In a college town like Boston, the athletic talent pool runs especially deep. From the very beginning to this day, Gentle Giant has sought workers from school sports teams, including rowing, rugby, football, hockey, wrestling etc. When you watch an athlete in the last 500 meters of a rowing race, the last period of a wrestling match, or the last lap of a mile race, you see someone in a severe oxygen deficit who is still giving 100%. Such are the people who *should* be and are working for us.

Today, with so many positions to fill across so many markets, we are proactive in our recruitment. Our connections with high school and college athletic directors and coaches have been extraordinarily fruitful. Those folks know which players have the right character and attitude. They also know who may be looking for work during the summer. A physically demanding job that also helps athletes stay in shape when they're not in regular competition is something both they and their coaches appreciate. Over the years, working summers for Gentle Giant has become something of a legacy for individual teams. Veterans of our company recommend us to new players.

I really believe that sports build character, and Gentle Giant's tradition of seeking out athletes has served us very well. So many of life's lessons are brought to the fore with immediacy in sports—the discipline it takes to master one's mind and body, the drive to surpass one's limits, the camaraderie and the caring that develops between people pulling together for the same goal. Athletes who play team sports move fluidly between follower and leadership roles—between taking direction and taking initiative. They want to win not because they're in love with victory, but because they're in love with being their best. And also, because in moments of supreme physical exertion, they are having the times of their lives.

One coach sent us a young woman who rowed for Boston University. She was a whirlwind of energy and creativity: a superstar who became a coach of our company's rowing team. Ultimately, she left, earned a master's degree, and became a biostatistician. But for eight months, we were able to put someone like that in front of our customers. How could that not make me proud? A team member who stayed longer—he is still with us—came from a less traditional form of athleticism. We found him at a local Parkour club. Practitioners of Parkour employ athleticism and improvisation to chart a sometimes gravity-defying course between two points across a complex environment. They can jump, run, climb, roll: whatever it takes to traverse the space as quickly and efficiently as possible. Players must be mentally and physically agile so they can quickly calculate optimal moves. It turns out that Parkour elegantly embodies the problem-solving aspect of moving. If you need to maneuver a six-foot credenza down a twisty staircase, you can't go wrong by thinking like a Parkour player. We benefit from having someone with this skillset on staff.

College rowers like myself were among the first people that I recruited for my startup moving company. Rowers make brilliant crew chiefs and movers. And that is not just because rowing is such a physically demanding sport, although that's part of it. What matters more is that rowers both think and train collectively. Knowing they are only as strong as their weakest teammate, they push one another while also pulling together. There's a choreography to the sport, much as there is a choreography to a well-executed move.

Ambitious people committed to excellence and achievement are unlikely to be planning to be movers for the rest of their lives. Many of our non-seasonal workers come to us during transitions. Some recent college graduates want to save money for grad school or to travel. Many are enrolled in courses and in training for a place on competitive teams. They want flexible work that allows them to come and go as opportunities arise. Some, such as teachers and other school system employees for example, are looking for well-paying summer jobs that keep them fit.

An important feature of our approach to recruiting is flexibility, allowing people to set their own work schedules. At Gentle Giant, we use software that allows movers to schedule themselves. That is very appealing to our people. It allows employees to take care of personal matters, such as school events, medical appointments, childcare or eldercare coordination, and taking courses. This has led to avoiding stress due to needing to be somewhere else by a certain time. We put reasonable guardrails in place, of course, to help prevent gaps. We ask that movers sign up for time slots 4 or 5 weeks in advance, and once they have set their schedule, they are committed.

Attracting Attention in Recruitment Rich Environments

Sports teams, of course, use scouts to identify talent. They are especially adept at spotting players with promise rather than with fully developed skills. At Gentle Giant, while we don't employ dedicated scouts, we do try to spend as much time as possible where our target employees congregate. That includes school job fairs and visits to sports teams and clubs, where we regularly make presentations about the company. We maintain a high profile at sporting events, which require movers to transport everything from bleachers to boats. It is no coincidence that Gentle Giant is the official mover for the Boston Marathon and the Head of the Charles Regatta, a two-day competition in which thousands of rowers compete for their clubs or schools.

The challenge at these events is attracting notice. The young people swirling around us have concerns other than checking out the moving industry. They are psyching themselves up to compete; exhilarated after a competition, or buoyant because they are out with their friends supporting their teams. And while a booth with representatives in logo-ed T-shirts passing out merch is a start, it is not exactly an attention magnet. Nor can it begin to demonstrate what it's like to work at Gentle Giant. We can't herd prospects onto a bus and drive them out to Harvard Stadium in order to give them a feel for our great traditions. But we have found a somewhat adequate alternative: Speed Stairs, a flight of 20 steps and a slide, constructed of steel and mounted on the back of a flatbed truck. We can't bring people to the stairs, but we can bring this version of stairs to them.

Since their debut at the 2008 Head of the Charles Regatta, the stairs have become a familiar and welcome sight at events around Boston. From the moment we roll in, we are surrounded by curious and eager people. Once we have their attention, we pose the Gentle Giant Challenge. Run up the stairs as quickly as you can, then come back down on the slide. Do that five times to qualify for the top prize of $500. Consolation prizes include T-shirts, water bottles, and bragging rights.

In addition to bringing the stairs to events, we set them up for local sports teams that want to host their own after-practice challenges. Everywhere we take them, the stairs draw people to us and start conversations. The Challenge offers the tiniest taste of our hallowed mornings at Harvard Stadium. More importantly, they provide a peek into the fun we have as a company and how much we expect of those who want to join us.

Great Contributors from Beyond Our Shores

Most of our year-round movers are qualified to serve as crew chiefs. But in the busy summer, we do not have as many of these highly qualified folks as we need. Hence, we must find seasonal crew chiefs—a demographic that does not exist in the United States. Fortunately, we are able to bring in returning workers from overseas who, during previous summers, have developed into crew chiefs. Back in 2001, I became aware of the H-2B program, which allows foreign nationals who are not immigrants to work in the United States on a seasonal basis. There is a crying need for these visas. Unfortunately, our Congress has capped the number at 166,000. Only 83,000 are available during the heavy moving season (of which moving takes an unknown fraction). Companies wanting to hire these people must submit proof that the jobs they're filling are, in fact, seasonal. Then they enter a lottery. The uncertainty creates a nightmare for businesses like ours. But it is also hard on visa applicants, who wait on pins and needles to learn whether they can start or return to a job that precisely fits their needs.

Just because applicants don't live here doesn't mean we're any less meticulous in evaluating them. We have traveled to countries (such as Lithuania, Romania and Honduras) to conduct interviews. We want to make sure every candidate meets our standards and speaks good English. Scores of these fantastic workers have returned year after year and been able to become crew chiefs. This enables us to hire more Americans during the summer. These Americans, usually college students, can return for as many as two years if we are lucky. However, there are never enough of them to form a stable group of expert high-season crew chiefs.

The Women of Gentle Giant

Moving is not work that attracts a lot of women. Nationally, around 5% of movers are women, according to the career site Zippia. Women have been among our greatest movers and crew chiefs, and I wish we could get more of them. Like many of their male counterparts, the women who work for us are extraordinary athletes: mostly rowers or rugby players, with some talented rock climbers in the mix. All the women who have applied to our company have been out to prove something to themselves and to the world. On the trucks, they focus intensely on doing the best possible job.

I remember one crew chief, Diana Landwehr, who was running an 11th floor move. Right at the end, the elevator broke down. "I guess we'll be coming back tomorrow," her crewmate said. But Diana knew we were booked solid the next morning.

"Grab your end," she said, tipping back the armoire she was moving. "We're going up the stairs."

We have had many heroic women like Diana. Unfortunately, women who take the job for a few summers—for the same reasons men do—are even less likely than men to make a career of it. Those who have remained at Gentle Giant have eventually left the trucks for other roles—in departments like accounting, sales, or quality control.

My first experience with women as movers was wholly serendipitous. It was September 1985. Hurricane Gloria was barreling toward Boston, expected to strike at noon the next day. We were too busy to postpone any jobs. So, I was frantically trying to rebook moves for later in the evening the day before the storm. Our crews got everyone on the schedule moved, except for a couple of jobs we arranged for 6 AM on the day of the hurricane. They were small ones. We figured we would finish long before Gloria descended.

But when we showed up at one of those last jobs, exhausted after working through the night, the customer turned us away. Originally, when she booked us, she had stressed how much pressure she was under to leave her home. Now, practically in tears, she explained that her mother was terrified of the storm and had made her promise she wouldn't try to move until it was over. We left and finished the other job. Then everyone went home. After the storm, at around 4 PM, the customer called and begged to be moved right then. Irritated though I was, I called one of the crew chiefs. His girlfriend answered and, as I had expected, informed me he was dead asleep. When I explained the situation, she said, "Let me call some of the other guys' girlfriends. Maybe we can do it."

That's how I ended up with three young women joining me at this customer's Cambridge home. A tree uprooted by the storm lay across the front doorstep. We had to saw off huge branches and lift everything over the trunk to get it all in the truck. The destination apartment, in Brookline, was on the seventh floor. The power was out. So: no elevator, and the stairwell was pitch-black. I was discussing the dilemma with the customer when one of the movers interrupted us. She and the other women had bought some candles at a nearby store and set them up on the landings.

"We're ready to go," she told me.

Since then, women movers have been a proud tradition at Gentle Giant. We've employed hundreds over the years and would have hired more if they'd applied. Unfortunately, women have never comprised more than 10% of the folks on our trucks. Occasionally, a customer will complain when a female mover comes to his house. He somehow thinks he's been short-changed, which, of course, is ridiculous. Far more common are the calls we get from people who say they were surprised to see a woman among their movers and delighted by that woman's performance.

If you run a business that's trying to attract more women applicants, your best bet is to encourage current women employees to enlist their friends. In the early 2000s, a woman from Ireland worked for us on the trucks. The next year, she came over again with four friends, all rugby players. Every one of them was fantastic.

I am both touched and grateful when amazing people choose to make their careers with us. But I am also happy to have been a way station for gifted athletes on their path to bright futures. It could be fun to send notes to customers who—completely unaware—consigned their La-Z-Boy recliners or Queen Anne dressers to the care of a future world champion. "We thought you'd like to know that Olympic medal winners Dan Walsh and Wyatt Allen, or World Cup competitor Katy Augustyn, or Miami Dolphins fullback Matt Kalapinski, or Boston Ballet soloist Sabi Varga was part of the team that moved you several years ago. We are confident they worked as hard for you as they have in subsequent endeavors."

Gentle Giant movers enjoying a summer party

CHAPTER FOUR

Developing Great Movers, Communicators, & Human Beings

A music teacher I knew called to tell me about one of her students: an incredibly gifted little girl whose family was so poor the teacher was giving her lessons for free. The mother was being forced to relocate from Dorchester to East Boston. They owned an enormous piano that someone had donated to them. As a favor, could I come and move it? I said we'd do it that night, after work. No charge.

This happened in winter, when Boston was an ice slick. I showed up at the job with Charlie Abrahams and Theirry Louvet, two super-strong dudes who rowed for Boston University. You might remember Theirry from a previous chapter. He had been recruited by BU (after competing for the French Olympic team) and was a genuine superstar. Few people learned as fast as he did. No one was kinder.

The family's new place was in a tiny tenement that you entered through a postage-stamp-size vestibule. A narrow, ancient, curving staircase made of horsehair plaster led to their apartment. With a single glance, I knew there was no way that piano was getting up those stairs. The windows in front were tiny. I went down the hall to check out the back bedroom. We were out of luck—the piano could not fit through any window. On hearing this news, the mother fell on her knees and buried her face on the bed. Then she raised her eyes and started to pray. She was imploring Jesus, Maria Y Jose to get that piano up those stairs. And I was thinking that Jesus, Maria Y Jose must have a list of higher priorities.

After several minutes of this, I heard a loud crash. I looked down the hall and saw a white cloud. The piano was at the top of the stairs. Theirry had overheard the woman praying.

"We are getting that piano up there," he had said to Charlie.

Together, they had got under the instrument and rammed it up the stairs, driving it into the plaster on a path to what Thierry called "victory."

Plaster dust was everywhere. I looked at the stairwell. It was destroyed.

"Theirry," I said. "Look what you've done."

"We answered her prayers," Theirry replied. "Rooty will fix it."

Theirry knew that, without the piano, this family would have suffered a terrible, sorrowful loss. He was just not prepared to let that happen.

As we were leaving, the mother didn't even say goodbye. She was still on her knees, thanking the Lord. I would have appreciated some of that gratitude directed at my crew. But they didn't seem to mind that God was stealing their thunder.

Treat All Workers Like Talent

The frontline workers are where the work seen by customers gets done. It is they who build the company's relationship with the public. Since frontliners are responsible for success, all of us who manage them ought to feel responsible for them. It is our job to develop the kinds of workers we would hate to lose and then to treat them so well that when they leave for a new career opportunity, they always do so with a sweet sorrow. It's a wonderful and poignant experience to congratulate an employee who, after learning so much at Gentle Giant, moves on to an exciting new opportunity. In these situations, there are always mixed feelings on both their part and mine—regret that they are leaving, and elation that they are "moving on up".

If you hire and invest in good people, many will inevitably move on to other opportunities. But others may stick around and rise in your organization. At industry events, my peers have occasionally given me a hard time for putting so much into an employee that I must surely have known would leave.

Well, it cuts both ways. I've also invested a lot in the wonderful people who stand ready and able to replace them. There's a burger-and-dog place in Tennessee called Pal's Sudden Service that invests in training fry cooks as though it expects them to create the next killer app. Reportedly, people say to the CEO, "What if you spend all that money on them and they leave?"

His response: "Suppose we don't, and they stay?"

Employers who wish to retain a highly skilled technical workforce know they must provide growth opportunities. By contrast, it is not uncommon for employers in service businesses to have low expectations of their employees. All employers, across all types of businesses, should view employees as "the talent pool". Employers in service industries, just like those in highly technical industries, should respect their workers—their talent pool—enough to discover and support their life goals.

Unfortunately, many service companies compete solely on price. Their business models rely on treating their people as commodities, and they proceed without regard for or interest in their employees' potential to rise to broader challenges. In such situations, companies don't invest in their people because they expect them, if they stick around, to do the same thing for years. The result is typically and, in my view, predictably, lousy customer service. Unless the customer is considered expendable, the development of frontline employees must be regarded as a fundamental business responsibility. When great employees move on, in their wake, they leave a business better, smarter, and more cohesive. At Gentle Giant, their exploits become part of the company's proud lore—an inspiration to workers who have not even had the opportunity to meet them.

Gentle Giant focuses on developing what are often called "the soft skills." Although we are in a heavy-lifting business, we have a workforce of highly skilled communicators with emotional intelligence who deserve the credit for our growth. We at Gentle Giant are also in the business of developing soft skills. We invest resources needed to attract, train, and retain an expanding workforce with outstanding abilities to empathize with customers.

By providing avenues for advancement through the development of these skills, I aimed to enhance satisfaction and enable professional and personal growth. I placed my bets on the premise that employees who appreciate Gentle Giant's environment of workplace satisfaction and personal advancement will go above-and-beyond, and tout us to their friends—and, later, to their own and their friends' children—long after leaving the company. It was obvious to me that our customers would automatically benefit from this type of workforce.

This strategy, I wagered, would allow us to succeed despite the ominous warnings that growth, in a service industry such as ours. inevitably involved quality slippage. Heeding my grandfather's advice—to guard vigilantly against bad-attitude people who would contaminate the workplace—remained and remains my guiding principle. My objective was, and is, to train first-rate people, and enable them to develop more first-rate people who, in turn, would develop more first-rate people. I envisioned, and continue to envision, a quality cascade. I knew, and know, that such an environment of excellence and camaraderie attracts great people. Great workers crave a work environment filled with other great, cooperative, helpful and supportive people. Great people want to join a team of fellow champions, with veterans as guiding role models. We committed to doing what was needed to keep the cascade of excellence uninterrupted as the number of employees needed to meet demand continued to expand.

Of course, we value greatly the awards and social media accolades that Gentle Giant has garnered over the years. But we cherish more the stacks of unsolicited letters and emails from our customers extolling what we have done for them. Certainly, these letters make us proud. But we cherish even more, and are even more proud of, our folders stuffed with letters from past employees, expressing gratitude for giving them a chance, a job, direction, new skills, self-confidence, motivation, a work ethic, or a future. These letters represent our legacy. As a father myself, perhaps even closer to my own heart are the notes from all the parents of our young employees thanking us for the same thing. These letters represent the core of our success.

Firm Push on Soft Skills

At the heart of Gentle Giant's employee development are three skills that improve effectiveness in any job and in professional and personal relationships. We train our people to: a) offer and receive feedback, b) manage conflict, and c) have the confidence to make decisions they personally believe are right. Almost always, those are the decisions that best serve the customer. If it turns out not to be the best decision, well, we learn from our mistakes, and no one will be admonished, even if we have to fix some plaster.

Our intense focus on these three core skills pays double dividends. First, our customers' moving experience is enriched by the unflappable good humor, enthusiasm, and proficiency of our movers. Second, we are teaching our movers the kinds of life skills that serve them well, regardless of what career path they ultimately choose. And our movers have gone on to great careers, including coaches, surgeons, lawyers, corporate executives, teachers, and, yes, our own in-house

Gentle Giant executives. We elevate performance and deepen the confidence of all those who leave us and those who stay, because they've come to see moving as a fulfilling career. Regardless of how long they stay with us, our frontline workers represent us in the best imaginable way. The satisfaction of knowing we helped shape the futures of exceptional individuals is an enormous bonus.

We start training hires in both "hard" moving and "soft" relational skills in their first two days at the company. In Boston, our orientation program, Gentle Giant 101, commences immediately after the Stadium run, followed by a big bacon-and-eggs breakfast. I do the honors, often joined by our CEO, Tom O'Gorman, and Vice President of Operations, Pat Inman. I begin by discussing our company's history and values. Then I ask the new people what they want to get out of the job. For many, this is the first time they've considered that they *can* get something other than a paycheck.

During my presentation, I prompt new team members to think about the broader context of their lives. I ask what, if anything, they would like to change about themselves? What, for them, would define success? And what would happiness look like? From there, we talk about the traits and behaviors that lead to fulfillment. For many of these people, the fact that the CEO of a $60 million company is taking an interest in their personal aspirations is mind-blowing. As Gentle Giant has grown, I've had to give up many responsibilities. But not the Stadium runs and not the orientations. I love them. And I love that my presence signals to these novices that they have stumbled into something more significant than a run-of-the-mill job.

During orientation, I also begin discussing the life skills—such as self-awareness and active listening—that will comprise much of their training with us. After years of obsessing over grades, test scores, and athletic achievements, many have never previously considered that less-measurable capabilities could affect their success. In the hundreds of notes that I've received from, and conversations I've had with former employees, it is those skills they most often reflect upon with gratitude.

In essence, we are teaching our people to be better communicators. Whether they're working with a partner to maneuver a bulky couch down a spiral staircase or calming a customer so afraid for her heirloom dishes that she is near to fainting, communication is at the core of every mover's—and every service worker's—job. Lou Insalaco, who worked for us from high school through medical school, told us about his residency interview. Most people on that professional track seek early jobs in related fields. But when the panel asked him about his life experiences, he talked about being a crew chief for Gentle Giant. He realized the skills he'd developed with us were more important than what he might have learned interning at a research lab. One of the interviewers, it turned out, was a customer of ours who was very familiar with our work. The leadership, empathy, and drive he had observed in Gentle Giant crew chiefs were exactly the traits he liked to see in doctors. Lou got the position. He is now on the faculty of Harvard Medical School and a surgeon in the Department of Otolaryngology at Mass Eye and Ear. He is known for his empathic bedside manner.

We all get a thrill when star athletes, master actors, and gifted orators demonstrate the heights to which their crafts can reach. The jobs of those who serve us—our movers, or waitstaff, or landscapers, etc.—are less prestigious, of course. But when we become great at what we do, it is because we have put our hearts, souls, brains, muscles, and empathic natures into becoming great. I promise a great surge of justifiable pride to anyone who plays a role in placing others at such a pinnacle. Hearts of both mentor and mentee will soar as the ranks of thrilled customers fill.

The Skills of Offering and Receiving Feedback

When I was a teenager and Dadden, my grandfather, was teaching me to drive, someone honked at me and I reacted with anger.

"Maybe he's an eejit," Dadden said about the honking driver. "But you should always look at yourself first. Do you think there is something you could have done a little better back there?"

Dadden was telling me what I, a teenager, was not quite ready to hear. Even though the blaring horn had annoyed me, I should think about how the incident could help me improve as a driver. Obviously, Dadden's words stuck with me, despite my resistance to them at the time. Eventually, I became a better driver and, as I developed into a leader, an ardent believer in feedback as perhaps the most valuable career development tool. Most of what I know about feedback—the things we coach people on at Gentle Giant—I've learned on the job.

I remember my first review after being hired as an engineer. I received mostly 6s on a 9-point scale. I was devastated. My reaction—knee-jerk defensiveness—was, as seen through the lens of my life's experience, unproductive in the extreme. Rather than being upset with my boss, I should have been asking him what I needed to do to improve. Knee-jerk defensive reactions are typical, in fact wholly predictable, among young people entering the work force. This leads to the temptation for supervisors to shy away from their responsibility to give feedback.

When delivering feedback, the top priority is to ensure you do not demoralize the recipient. Giving positive feedback comes first. Giving critical input comes later. When our employees finish a job, they've given it everything they've got. They should not be needled about some minor thing that went wrong. Positive feedback builds credibility and trust—a process essential in helping a person develop. In such a supportive environment, people are more willing to listen to and benefit from critical feedback.

Ideally, the supervisor will wait for an opportunity to deliver the feedback as coaching rather than criticism. For example, if he wants to address a crew chief about the less-than-perfect state of his truck, he won't do it after he has just completed a challenging move. Instead, he will have a word when the mover is headed out on another job. That way, he is not rubbing the person's nose in it. He is saying, "Here's what we want." Not, "You didn't do what we want."

When managers do give constructive feedback, we coach them to be a little bit self-deprecating. For the recipient, it goes down more easily if the manager doesn't act as if he is passing judgment from on high. Also, we warn managers not to assume their suggestions will take effect instantly. People don't always absorb everything that's said to them, particularly in the logistically challenging situation of a move.

We regard training for receiving feedback as equally important as training for offering it. We want our people to ask for feedback explicitly and do so in the right spirit. That means they've got to convince their managers that they really want it and won't get upset or make things uncomfortable by reacting defensively. If, after a job a mover asks the crew chief, "How am I doing?", the crew chief might respond with "fine" or "great." That doesn't mean he hasn't noticed room for improvement. We advise people to seek feedback by first convincing their supervisors that they won't be upset if they receive a candid, critical reply. One question we suggest they ask is: "Tell me one thing I could have done better." Or, like James in the story that introduced Chapter 3, they can express their own doubts. That makes it a lot easier for the supervisor to introduce the constructive criticism the employee needs.

Naturally, employees don't always agree with what the supervisor says. But that doesn't mean they can just dismiss it. With any piece of feedback, there's a 99% chance of at least 1% truth. We want people to always look for that 1%, treat all feedback as a gift, and not push against it. This is how to keep the channels open. When I talk to new hires, I often pose this question: "What do you say to someone who offers you feedback that you happen to know is not accurate?" Recently, when I asked this to a group of ten of them, only one had the right answer:

"You tell them, 'Thank you,'" she said.

When you say that, you are building a relationship in which people are not afraid to give you critical feedback.

Many companies reserve most of their feedback for annual reviews. That is the absolute worst time to deliver it. Feedback must be part of coaching throughout the year, and the employee shouldn't have to wait months to hear improvement advice. Nothing said about performance or prospects should ever come as a surprise at an annual review. Moreover, during such reviews employees may not even take in what they are being told, regardless of whether improvements are being requested. The reviewee's mindset is anxiously focused on the prospect of promotions and raises, making it challenging to process other input.

We don't do annual reviews at Gentle Giant. Instead, feedback is continuous. Coaching someone into a new role is very satisfying when that person is a feedback sponge. However, a trap I have fallen into is not having the judgement to know when to back off and let the person fly solo. This kind of micromanagement can disrupt anyone's ability to take feedback. A person needs room to grow into taking full responsibility and to start learning from their mistakes.

In the early days, I didn't worry much about what I said to workers or how I said it. But as the company grew, people started viewing me as more of a big deal than I thought myself to be. Every comment I made, even relatively minor constructive criticism, carried far more impact than I was conscious of, more than it would have if it had come from a co-worker or supervisor. I became acutely aware of this phenomenon when I was complimenting Gordan Rowell, one of our greatest crew chiefs. A very grateful and delighted customer called me just after his crew had left her job. The ornamental trees on her driveway had been damaged by the moving company used by the previous owners. She had dreaded the possibility of additional damage. However, before she was even aware of the arrival of Gentle Giant, the crew had proactively protected the trees by tying back the branches.

I went down to meet the truck and relayed the customer's appreciation to Gordon. And then I said,

"Let me get out of the way so you can finish cleaning up your truck."

The next day, somebody asked me,

"Why did you give Gordon such a hard time about cleaning his truck?"

I was gob-smacked. Movers are supposed to handle the cleanup at their job sites. But on that day, in order to enable a crew member to be on time for a concert, Gordon decided to do the clean up at the yard. Before he could start, he saw me coming over to him, and worried that I would fault him for this minor violation of protocol. Given his mindset, he misinterpreted my comment about the truck, and my compliment, if it registered at all, did not give him the boost I intended.

Now I have learned that when I, or any other top executive, see something to correct, I must refrain from comment. It is always better to hold your tongue. But that doesn't mean the situation should be ignored. At our company, when I notice a problem, I inform the relevant supervisor. All our supervisors know that timing and context are important. They do not just run up to an employee and reprimand him.

Just as criticism from a CEO can have an outsize negative effect, the leader's praise contributes enormously to the workplace culture. Many long-time employees have recalled encouraging words from me at the start of their tenures. What great benefits—to work-place satisfaction and employee loyalty—I have reaped from whatever words of support I took the time to give. At Gentle Giant we expect managers to be liberal with positive feedback, thereby building trust with employees. As problems arise, we can rely on those nurtured relationships to set things right.

Developing Decision Makers

The professional development aspect of a job at Gentle Giant starts on day one. Someone joins us without any expectation beyond working hard and making money. Then the leadership stuff sneaks up. After a year or two, he finds himself running a move: responsible for a couple of $80,000 trucks, a quarter-million dollars' worth of belongings, and a team of people looking for guidance. We start preparing movers to assume responsibility before they even aspire to it. It is from the very beginning that workers are treated like talent. One day, they are sitting in orientation. Two days later, they may be on a truck with the crew chief, sharing their opinion on how to handle a tricky maneuver.

Moving jobs are all different, and challenges can be logistically complex, emotionally taxing, or borderline surreal. Our people must be great improvisers, comfortable solving problems and making decisions on the fly. That means they must feel empowered. And they have to believe that the right thing to do is always the compassionate thing to do. The professional thing to do. The Gentle Giant thing to do. We ask them to consider what they would do if it was their company. We tell them we trust them to keep our values in mind and make the right decisions.

Once, we were moving a very high-end customer out of Back Bay. He had a new mattress that had cost at least $2,500, back then a very high-end mattress. The crew got it loaded. But while they were working, it started to rain. A real deluge. Turns out there was a small leak in the truck that no one had noticed. When we got to the customer's new home, the mattress was wet.

Customers react differently to things like that. Some might say not to worry about it and pull out a fan. Some might yell at you. The crew chief on this job, John Dalton, didn't wait to find out what the customer would do. On the spot, he made his decision. He called our quality control manager. "The mattress got wet. We need to replace it," he said. "Here's the make and model number." A new mattress arrived at the site before the job was finished.

If the crew chief had waited for authorization from his supervisor or a manager, that could have taken hours or days. He wasn't going to carry even a slightly damp mattress into that customer's home, and he was not going to make the customer wait. That would not have been consistent with the Giant HEART. If you can't trust workers to make those kinds of decisions, either you've hired wrong or trained wrong. No customer should be forced to wait for the back office to fix things. No worker should be made to doubt a decision made in the customer's best interest.

To reliably achieve such outcomes, you must take fear out of the equation. When employees don't have to worry about being called on the carpet for making an on-the-spot decision, they can calmly act with the HEART values in mind. It is a great feeling for a crew to complete a complicated job successfully. They should be congratulated for such accomplishments. When workers are called out for some minor problem, it is a morale buster. Removing the fear of repercussions is ingrained in Gentle Giant culture. Creating this penalty-free atmosphere prioritizes honesty and is strongly in the company's and our customers' interests. (At some companies, if a mover makes a mistake—particularly one that costs the company money—they are admonished or even docked some portion of their bonus fund.)

Taking Down the Temperature

It's easy to be nice to nice people, and most of our customers are nice. It's in the tough cases that our crews get to test their conflict-resolution skills. Moving is often stressful for customers. Sometimes, a customer can be so anxious that they cannot calm down sufficiently to discuss a challenging situation. They can reject—almost as a knee-jerk reaction—solutions being offered by the crew. Giants need to know how to resolve those conflicts without getting ruffled and/or losing sight of the customer's right to respect.

It would be natural to get your hackles up when someone, especially someone under stress, keeps arguing and rejecting all proposed solutions. It is perhaps predictable that one would despair of ever being able to resolve such an impasse. But this is exactly the type of situation where our Giant HEART value of respect becomes indispensable. You can't resolve a conflict in a genuine, non-patronizing way if you don't respect the other person. And if you don't respect the other person, the other person will easily perceive that lack of respect. The more stressed the customer becomes, the harder it becomes to retain the customer's trust. It is in these situations that Gentle Giant's focus on developing people skills serves both the company and the customer in the best possible ways.

Teaching conflict resolution requires instilling confidence. When I started as a mover, handling disputes gave me immense fulfillment and confidence in my own skin. I learned how to talk to people in ways that influenced their viewpoints. When I disagreed with someone, I never explained why they were wrong. Instead, I tried to understand why they thought they were right. I came to believe I could turn anyone around so they could see that we were on the same side.

Probably the most common disputes our movers encounter are about money. When the company started, I was booking all the jobs myself. People would ask for estimates; and I'd tell them I couldn't predict the future. It would cost what it cost. But I could guarantee that we would do the job faster and better than anybody else. Customers went along with that because they were dealing directly with the owner. As the company grew and we hired a sales force, that approach was no longer sustainable.

So, now we give estimates. And 90% of jobs will conform to those. But, sometimes, our estimates will be too low. That often happens because the customer is so completely disorganized that he didn't do what he said he would in preparation. Our folks arrive at the job site and find that the promised yard sale did not take place. Or the customer had said he would organize and pack his own possessions but did not complete the process.

For example, an estimate is $4,000, and the crew chief can see that it will likely cost $2,000 more. The crew chief has been trained to wait until the movers—working with their usual remarkable energy and efficiency—have won the customer's trust. He then explains why the estimate is low or simply acknowledges that our assessment is off. Many customers will immediately understand and accept the additional cost. The salesperson will already have told them that estimates are not written in concrete. They know they are paying by the hour.

Sometimes, though, the customer will push back.

"Oh my God! Six thousand dollars? I budgeted $4,000! That's crazy! Ridiculous!"

"Well, that was just the estimate," our crew chief will respond. "Surely you realized that the charge could be more than that."

"Not by $2,000, I didn't!"

The crew chief wants to avoid being refused payment when he presents the bill. So, for example, he might negotiate a price the customer is comfortable with, say, $5,000. Reaching that number requires reducing the scope of the job. That means customers must agree to use their own vehicles to move some items that are time-consuming to pack.

I've been in that type of situation many times. I've had to explain to the customer that, to stay within budget, we'll have to leave without getting all her belongings into the truck. Most times, they experience a change of heart. "Why don't you just move all of these pictures, lamps, and plants?" they'll say. "I think I will just pay the extra money." I'm never surprised when people do that.

In a few situations, someone has tried to wrangle a discount after the job was done. One woman, who was leaving her husband, hired us to move her without his knowledge. The crew loaded her belongings, left for the offload, and stopped for lunch on the way. While they were dining, the customer called Jon Powell, the crew chief, and asked him to bring everything back to the onload site. She and her husband had reconciled.

The crew drove back and restored all her belongings to their original locations. Then Jon presented the bill. The customer questioned whether she should have to pay it all, given that they hadn't delivered anything to the specified offload. She tried to get off the hook by promising to use us in the future. Jon politely explained that things didn't work that way and left with the entire amount.

There have been times—rare, fortunately, but memorable—when a customer got so mad that they lashed out at us. When it's not justified, that feels terrible. Even when a customer is being unreasonable, we would always prefer to negotiate a resolution, even if at a loss, rather than leave an angry customer dangling. When someone is angry for a valid reason, the remedial process is, by comparison, smooth sailing. We immediately direct our efforts to making things right. We once moved a woman from Washington D.C. to Los Angeles. When her things arrived, they were the wrong things. She and her sister had both stored their possessions in our D.C. facility. We mixed them up. It was a massive mistake—and it was our mistake. Oh, she was mad! Within an hour, we had a truck on its way with two drivers. We broke a few laws to get her things to her in record time. (I'm confident no regulators will be reading this book.) In the end, she was thrilled with Gentle Giant.

Some crew chiefs can work for years without ever having an unhappy customer. Then suddenly they find themselves in a situation where things have gone wrong on a big move. It's easy to see why they might get flustered and forget the estimate. Before they know it, they've finished the job, and the customer resists payment. We tell our people: you still can bring it around to a happy outcome. But only if you take control of the situation. And you absolutely can control it. You have the skills. You have the authority. Stay calm, have HEART.

Over the years, we've tried different approaches, including occasional role-playing exercises, to teach people how to have difficult conversations. (My father was a playwright. I understand that inhabiting a role can change how you think.) We've even had an improvisation troupe come in a few times. The goal is always to push our employees out of comfort zones. We condition them to respond in the moment to situational cues rather than adhere to a rigid script.

Tales In and Out of Class

Crew chiefs are the principal conduits for our Gentle Giant HEART. They are the people I trust to uphold the standards. Therefore, developing great crew chiefs is a top priority. We give people authority, trust them, build their confidence, and treat them with respect. At Gentle Giant, we make employees proud to be movers. (And at the same time, we are preparing them for lives where they can be anything.) Growth opportunities are available to everyone at Gentle Giant. Our trainers, most of them former crew chiefs, know that one of their most important duties is identifying those with the potential to grow into the crew chief role. All we have built at Gentle Giant—our reputation for extraordinary service, our ability to rise to any challenge, our commitment to being kind, empathetic and respectful to people who might be facing horrible loss and/or stress, and our iron-clad determination to always act with integrity and honesty—rests on the shoulders of our crew chiefs.

Because our most important goal is to ensure that the standards we set are consistently passed along to each new hire, the prime focus of our training is on developing great crew chiefs. The intensity of this training is reflected in all aspects of both "hard" and "soft" skill development—from leadership and conflict resolution to technical performance. No one is promoted to crew chief without the endorsement of the trainers. In fact, no one is promoted to any position at Gentle Giant until trainers vouch for them. Our people know that, "Can I have more pay?" is never the right question. The right question is, "I need more pay, and what can I do to make that happen?" The answer is usually some combination of new skill acquisition and performance benchmarks.

Some of the most effective learning takes place in group conversations of roughly 10 participants: a mix of those who have the job and others who soon will. They share concerns, experiences, and strategies. And, of course, stories. As you have already gathered, Gentle Giant story telling is at the heart of the Giant culture. New stories are continually being added to the old ones. Think of the stories as our legal tender. The more stories one has—of wonderful customers, of eccentric customers, of hyper-challenging requests, of floods and blizzards, of extraordinary occurrences of all type—the closer one gets to the status of a legend Giant. And "richer in lore" translates to richer in wisdom. These stories, as they get passed along, become great teaching tools. The tradition of using stories to impart wise teachings is central to many (maybe all?) cultures. At Gentle Giant, we are proud of our huge, evocative, amusing, empathy-inducing, informative collection of stories. It is an essential tool for our employee development.

Customers often comment on how calm our people stay, even when, by any objective standard, the situation is nerve-racking. I believe the explanation lies at least in part in the storytelling. First, stories of past triumphs over adversity instill confidence that the present challenge, whatever it may be, will be overcome. Secondly, and I believe crucially, when the job is done, telling fresh stories to sympathetic ears provides a pressure-release valve (in addition to providing a new learning opportunity for the listeners). The therapeutic value of talking through an experience is well known, and the Giant storytelling sessions let our workers decompress.

Our classes emphasize the importance of empathy and good communication on the job. We also urge people to practice what they learn outside the job. Employees are coached on using these skills in low-risk personal situations. Trainers might use an interaction with a sales clerk at a service station convenience store as an example. Ask how his day is going and hold his gaze for a moment, indicating that you are waiting for an answer. Try to create a moment of connection with that person.

Trainers will also point out how these practices can help elevate exchanges with your friends and family. Ask questions and listen carefully to the answers. Don't make assumptions. Respond instead of reacting. Analyze your own thinking. Instead of yelling at your kid for spending too much money, consider why you are so upset and whether your reaction is proportional. Focus on getting to that good conclusion. Employees often express appreciation for how the lessons from Gentle Giant help in everyday life.

Our employees, just like employees everywhere, obviously focus on how these classes affect their careers and compensation in the immediate future. There should never be any mystery about who gets ahead and why. Without crystal-clear criteria, people will grumble about favoritism or claim they've been judged unfairly, which, in turn, will cause severe damage to morale. To avoid that, we've created a job ladder that spells out, in purely objective measures, what employees at each rung must do to reach the next. If you're a mover who wants to become a senior mover or a senior mover who wants to be a master mover, the ladder tells you exactly what technical and interpersonal training and skills are needed to get you there. Each step up that ladder comes with a pay increase. As we watch our people strive to climb that ladder, we know we have the right people.

In many other companies, when the hiring and probationary process fails to identify poor performers, employers resort to incentives to encourage improvement. To me, at the core of incentive programs is an assumption that at least some proportion of the workforce is not performing at their very best. Gentle Giant has built a company predicated on the premise that everyone does their very best and trusts everyone else to do the same. I do not want to implement policies that intrinsically undermine that core ethos of Gentle Giant. Employers who implement incentive programs do so because of the (fairly well) founded premise that incentives can cause poor performers to "up their game" for personal (rather than team or customer) gain. But what about great performers? They are already giving their best, so any implication that they can, or should, perform better, inevitably risks being either a subtle insult or a formula for burnout. When you have engaged, enthusiastic employees, incentives can undermine intrinsic motivation by demoralizing your best team players who will not thrive in a "what's in it for me" workplace culture.

The Giant Steps

As I have explained, Gentle Giant does not conduct annual performance reviews. (Feedback is constant and an annual review is absolutely the worst time to deliver it.) In our system, each employee has a semi-annual conversation with their supervisor that covers a few standard topics, such as development goals. We call these conversations Giant Steps. We ask employees about their life objectives and how we can help them get there, even if "there" means a future outside Gentle Giant.

To us, the Giant Steps are an important career check-in. We want to know how things are going, both personally and professionally, and what we can do to help. The Giant Steps are essential to the health of the company. Holding ongoing, intentional conversations safeguards against overlooking an employee's struggles or discontent. Squeaky wheels get the oil, yes, but at Gentle Giant, we aim to make sure that the silent wheels get the oil they deserve. We don't want to lose people due to our own inattentiveness.

We once paid a high price for letting the Giant Steps process slip during one of our very busy periods. We had an excellent employee in mind to head up a branch of our business. We knew he had qualifications in high demand in the high-tech industry. But we weren't worried because he had previously told us that he was happy on the trucks. But, lo and behold, the employee got a high-tech job offer. Out the door he went. The Giant Steps might have signaled that he was eyeing an exit. That would have allowed us to make sure he understood his options before making a final decision. We might have been able to retain him. The Giant Steps minimizes the likelihood of being caught off guard like this.

It is important to guard against managers deceiving themselves into believing that employees who receive career development training have been given a gift or that the company is doing them a big favor. There is an arrogance to that way of thinking. It's how unpaid internships got created. Yes, I do love hearing former Giants express gratitude to me for how Giant training has influenced their lives. But whatever benefits our employees get from us, I always feel the balance of benefits tilts decidedly in Gentle Giant's favor.

CHAPTER FIVE

The Art of Customer Service

In 1989, we were moving two sisters, whose families—large, lots of little kids—lived together under one roof. The husbands were at work. I had moved these people a few times in the past and knew they were not overly polite. They also seemed to live in a state of perpetual pandemonium. I had given them a very high estimate hoping they would hire a different mover.

"We have another estimate from another moving company that's half of that," they informed me.

"Wonderful!" I said, "I would take that if I were you."

"But we want you," they insisted.

I stuck to my guns on the price. They booked anyway. I think it was because they knew from their previous moves with us that they would be treated with respect. We loaded two-and-a-half trucks, reserving room in the last truck for the furniture of the sisters' bedridden grandmother. I had met the grandmother on previous moves. (On one occasion, the family insisted I move her furniture to a room at New England Baptist Hospital, where she was scheduled for an extended stay. Not surprisingly, the hospital kicked us out.)

This time around, the sisters asked if we could save her room until the end so she could sleep as long as possible. When the time came, our crew loaded up the grandmother's dresser, chairs, and other furniture. But the bed posed a problem because she was still in it. The sisters suggested we just move it that way. They wanted us to load Granny into the back of the truck, with the furniture and boxes.

We had multiple objections. I decided to start with the most practical one. We would have to tip the bed to get it out of the room, I explained to the sisters. When we did that, their grandmother would fall off. They pointed to the straps we use to secure furniture and suggested we use them. "Is that OK with you, Granny?" they asked the woman, who by this time was awake and listening with great interest.

I proceeded to the next objection: "It's illegal to carry even live animals in any enclosed truck." That should have more than precluded the grandmother. But one of the sisters shot back, "We're only going a mile. The cops don't have x-ray vision."

At Gentle Giant, we will do almost anything to accommodate our customers. Often, we can resolve challenges just by carrying things farther or working longer. This situation, however, required both ingenuity and access to unusual resources. That day we had both.

One of our teammates held a second job as a medical technician. We called him. He explained to his boss there that he needed an ambulance for a family situation and managed to get permission to transport an elderly woman. Then he drove it over to the job site. Two of our guys lifted the grandmother onto a stretcher and loaded her into the back. At the new home, we set up Granny's furniture first. Then we carried her up to the bed and left her, as we had found her.

Satisfaction Guaranteed

People talk about the wisdom of creating low expectations and exceeding them. Better, surely, to create high expectations and exceed those. The world's premier hotels and restaurants always strive to do this. At Gentle Giant, we don't just create high expectations—we guarantee they will be met.

In 1992, we did a move for Gary Loveman, an economist and professor at Harvard Business School. Gary was so impressed by our performance that he invited me to sit in on some of his classes and then took me to lunch at Harvard Business School to talk about Gentle Giant's practices.

"Everything you are doing is great," he said to me. "But you should also offer a guarantee. That will set you apart from the competition and solidify your customer base."

We could offer a money-back guarantee for the whole job if every move cost the price of a pair of boots from Nordstrom's. But moving can be a significant expense. Jobs can run into the tens of thousands of dollars. So full refunds are not practical. Therefore, in response to Gary's advice, we devised the Gentle Giant version of a guarantee of service. We offer a money-back guarantee for the performance of each individual member of the moving crew: the packer, driver, and local or long-distance movers. If the customer has the slightest complaint about any team member, we calculate the amount charged for that person's work and refund all of it.

On the rare occasions when customers call in that guarantee, we don't argue with them, even if they are not being reasonable. Someone once complained that we sent her a trainee in his first week. Never mind that the aggregate experience of the crew exceeded 40 years. One customer was unhappy with the performance of the single greatest crew chief in Gentle Giant's history. I'm sure that complaint was complete nonsense. Still, we never push back. We smile, hold our peace, and pay up. When you hire a mover, the most important consideration shouldn't be the price. It should be who the company dispatches to your home. Guaranteeing satisfaction for each crew member forces us to be very careful about whom we dispatch. When salespeople tell potential customers about our policy, it communicates the company's great pride and trust in every Gentle Giant.

Setting Expectation at "Delightful"

In many ways, our employees and customers can be seen as dancing together. Each job is a new and different dance. Going into it, neither side knows exactly what the dance will be. Partners respond in real time to the music, to one another's movements, and to their emotions. At Gentle Giant, our movers must figure out how to coordinate the choreography. For that, employees must be compassionate. They must be emotionally intelligent. They must be comfortable with improvisation. All the while, they must maintain a dizzyingly high level of physical activity.

Few people expect gold-medal performance from a moving company. Yet businesses like ours have endless opportunities to surprise customers and, in the process, create true delight. And I don't just mean "do a perfect job." If all you do is avoid making mistakes, most of the time, the customer won't even notice. If someone asks about the move, they will reply that it was "fine."

We want them to say, "Oh, wow, I was delighted! They were the nicest people! I loved having them in my home." Customer satisfaction isn't good enough for us. We aim for delight. To my mind, delight is another creature altogether. Delight communicates joy spiced with a pinch of surprise. We aim for "delight."

It is especially gratifying when someone who hired a competitor expresses awe at Gentle Giant's performance. One clear example comes from one of our jobs in the mid-'80s. The Giants had begun moving out a customer before 8 AM. By noon, we were offloading at his new home on Commonwealth Avenue, a grand Boston promenade lined with stately brownstones. That same day, another family was moving out of the adjacent brownstone. While we were hauling the last boxes up to the third floor, the neighbor's crew was still struggling to load their truck, even though, as we found out later, they'd begun at roughly the same time as we had. Our customer was ecstatic. But the neighbor was, of course, crestfallen and came to talk to me. She was flabbergasted by our speed. She fretted that her own movers might still not be finished by midnight.

Later, I dropped by the Muddy to brag. My ego shrank a bit when a chorus pointed out the caliber of my colleagues on that job—two movers who were also Olympians. Still, on that day, I knew we had been at our best. I imagined our customer—ensconced in her new home, marveling at the lack of wear and tear on both her possessions and her nerves—mentally adding the Giants to her list of "great-decisions-I-have-made."

In the Preamble, I cited "above-and-beyond" as one of our Giant HEART values. I count three levels of above-and-beyond service. At the first level, our movers are always on the lookout for thoughtful ways to make people's lives a little brighter. Often, they will call ahead to ask whether customers would like them to bring coffee. (After all, the customer's coffee machine will be packed away.) One customer asked a crew member how to buy a Gentle Giant shirt. We don't sell branded gear, at least not yet. But the mover had our office ship one of our shirts to the customer.

When movers learn something personal about a customer that they can act on, they do just that. A packer once overheard a customer's daughter say that the next day—moving day—was also her elderly mother's birthday. The moving team showed up with a cake and a song. Most people wouldn't do that for a friend. How amazing, then, the customer thinks that a moving company could be so thoughtful. There is a key to everyone's heart, we remind our people. It's up to them to find it.

The second level of above-and-beyond service involves responding expeditiously and with good grace when a job turns out to be more challenging than anyone anticipated. Customers might ask for special accommodation because their building double-booked the loading dock, or because their cats got spooked and are hiding somewhere in the furniture. Our teams have had to scale 7 flights of stairs when the elevator is broken. We've worked through the night on moves that have "blown up" and couldn't be rescheduled. We do not judge or blame our customers if, in the stress and chaos of preparing for a move, they forget something important, such as reserving use of their building's freight elevator. It's our job to get that move done and to do so in a way that eases the customer's anxiety as much as possible.

Heroics and ingenious problem solving, the third level of above-and-beyond, are sometimes called for, as in the case of the elderly lady who needed an ambulance. We once moved a couple out of a sprawling loft in a converted industrial building that was slated for demolition. The huge freight elevator was on its last legs and well past its mandatory inspection date. By the time we arrived, the customer had already stuffed it with his belongings.

I was the crew chief on that job. I told the guy it might be too much weight. The customer, insisting it was fine, stepped inside and pushed the button. The elevator dropped into the basement. There, it expired, with the doors locked shut, and the customer trapped inside.

This situation could rightly be considered within the purview of first responders. But it goes without saying that a crew committed to above-and-beyond service did not abandon a panicked customer crammed with half his belongings in an elevator. Our movers climbed down the shaft and removed part of the elevator roof to extract the customer. Then, we passed a truckload of boxes up through the elevator roof to the floor above and out through the loading dock.

Another crew was working on the day of Christmas Eve, racing a Nor'easter that was bearing down on the region. We urged the customer to postpone, but they were adamant. The move had to be on that day. Because the couple hadn't done the packing they had intended, things took longer than expected, and the team didn't arrive at the new place until around 3 PM. They were met by the driveway from hell—incredibly long and steep, with a sharp turn next to a forested drop-off. It was getting dark. The snow was sheeting down, making the going even more treacherous.

Our two huge trucks would have struggled to make that turn in the best of weather. As it was, the crew chief, Robert Leaver, worried they would end up at the bottom of the cliff. The team brainstormed. Two movers owned 4-wheel-drive vehicles: a pick-up truck and a Ford Explorer. They went home to retrieve them and then used them to shuttle everything up the drive, from the trucks to the house. Because visibility was so poor, they communicated using walkie-talkies to avoid the nightmare of the vehicles meeting each other as they went up or down the hill.

That crew used the type of above-and-beyond service described above to mitigate a disaster during a Nor'easter, but sometimes the result of this type of heroism is just pure joy. One customer, leaving his longtime home, spoke wistfully about a 700-pound rock in the front yard that had served as the backdrop for years' worth of family photos.

"You guys couldn't move that boulder by any chance?" he asked, more in jest than in hope. We had two type-A crew chiefs on that job. They answered, practically in unison: "Of course, we can move that boulder!" Which—with considerable effort—they did.

A few hours' hard work on our part can produce years of happiness. How gratifying for our employees, who, at the end of a job, can tell themselves, "Today I performed wonders for my customer." It's great when that is appreciated. But even if taken for granted, a crew can still feel great about having a new addition to the Giant lore.

Enthusiasm Carries the Day

The "E" in Giant HEART stands for enthusiasm. As long as jobs progress smoothly, do customers really care that the folks they've hired are happy and excited to be there? I would say yes. First because emotions are contagious. Customers immediately sense the energy, enthusiasm, and goodwill of movers who show up on time, smiling, ready to attack the job. They need our employees to do something for them. But they also need reassurance. They want optimism and good vibes. Our movers express enthusiasm through their interactions with one another and with the customer. They may chat with them for a moment. Pause to ask about the subject of a painting they admire. Laugh and encourage each other as they pass in the driveway or on the stairs. In that way, they're a bit like flight attendants. The more relaxed and upbeat they are, the less customers worry.

It helps that enthusiasm is also contagious within the crew. I'm thinking of sports again, where team members compete but also have fun and push one another to greater achievements. Customers appreciate that. It is gratifying to see their job tackled by cheerful, energized people who genuinely like each other. They get a better experience from a team that approaches the work less as a burden to be endured than as an invigorating challenge.

It is important, however, that our movers do not make assumptions and carefully read the customer. One person might get a charge from joining in the camaraderie. Another might be standoffish. One mover told me, when I hired him, that his greatest strength was connecting with customers. And sure, he was a very charismatic guy. But he trotted out the same schtick for people who wanted to be charmed as for those who needed comfort. You shouldn't do a stand-up comedy routine for a person whose mother has just died. You've got to "read the room"—meet customers where they are.

There are right ways and wrong ways to be playfully enthusiastic. We did a move that included mannequins. Our mover removed a mannequin from the dressing room, and as he passed by the customer, he gave her a big smile and, in just a few steps, waltzed the mannequin out the door. Mover and customer shared a brief, lighthearted moment. A connection was made. Contrast that with a mover who might act without humor in the customer's presence but later is seen out the window, waltzing across the lawn on the way to the truck. Lighthearted humor in the first situation—risk of a damaged reputation in the second.

When a customer is wholeheartedly willing to join in the fun, the results can be magical. During a casual exchange with one of our movers, Joel Adams, a customer let slip that she had once pursued a career in show business.

"Do you want to do some acting now?" Joel asked her.

The crew chief on that job was Henry Farrell, a wonderful mover from Ireland, who was a real practical joker. For instance, Henry liked to hide in wardrobe boxes and jump out. Joel saw a chance to turn the tables on him. The customer had an old triple-dresser in the garage that she wanted us to put out on the curb for disposal.

"We'll carry it up the ramp as if we're going to load it," Joel told her. "Then we'll drop it just as Henry is coming out of the house. And you get really angry at him."

The movers went up the ramp, tilting the dresser forward, and the drawers were sliding out. Then they stumbled a little.

"Guys! Guys!" cried Henry, as he made a dash to catch the item as it crashed to the ground.

The customer came out. She was yelling, "What have you done? Who are these lunatics you've brought me!" Henry was apologizing right and left. But the customer could not keep up the charade. She cracked a smile. The crew gave her a round of applause. For those few minutes, that customer was a Gentle Giant.

Enthusiasm is also important because it suggests hustle. An enthusiastic crew is excited to get started. They are itching to attack the job. By contrast, someone who is dragging or taking a lot of breaks does not inspire confidence that the cost per hour is good value. A lethargic performance shows a lack of respect for the customer's time and money, an unforgivable transgression in the Gentle Giant world.

At Gentle Giant, we are always mindful of giving the customer the most efficient service possible. For example, on a local job, if a tight load in one truck is anticipated, it may save the customer money if we use two trucks. The cost of an extra truck may be less than the extra time required to achieve a tight load in a single truck. The two-truck scenario allows for time savings both in the loading and unloading phases of the job. On the other hand, in a long-distance move, when a higher proportion of wages is for time spent driving, the more cost-efficient plan will almost certainly be the tightest loading possible. Maximizing the cost benefit to the customer is the goal.

Sometimes, really great movers make things look so easy that people fail to notice how smoothly things are progressing. Sometimes a remark from a crew member, such as "We are lucky we have Dave preparing your China cabinet today. He is a master!" may serve to spotlight a colleague's performance. A mover might even indulge in a bit of theater: doing something that looks dramatic but—to us—is no big deal. For example, people gasp when they see a Giant standing on a rooftop five stories above the sidewalk, leaning out to swing a large piece of furniture through an open window. (A safety harness means there's no risk. But most onlookers won't notice that.) In the company's early days, I occasionally would carry a piano up a staircase on my back. The TV news magazine *Chronicle* filmed that feat for a segment about jobs no one would want.

My introduction to the power of theater also involved a piano. Many years ago, I was working with a new hire to haul one up three flights of concrete steps to a house on a hill. This guy, newly hired, was the brother of one of my best movers. He had been a basketball player but had become out of shape. Every time he pushed up under the piano, he roared. It sounded so strange it made me cringe. And the customer heard every bellow.

Embarrassed, I tried to get out of there quickly after the customer paid the bill. But she stopped me. "That guy with you was incredible," she said. "Is he a power lifter?" Then she handed me a $100 bill. "Would you please give him this from me?" she asked. Of course, the new mover's theatrics were unintentional. But in the customer's eyes, his vocal eruptions led her to believe he had done something surprising.

Finally, enthusiasm can turn a bad situation around. When a customer behaves negatively, I generally coach the crew chief to say something like, "I get the feeling you are not happy with how things are going." That encourages the customer to speak up about what's troubling her. Nine times out of ten, it has nothing to do with us. Maybe her child is sick or she's having a hard time at work. Whatever the circumstances, our movers have the opportunity to empathize, build a connection, and assure the customer that they will put forth 100% effort.

Courtesy: Yes. Respect: YES!

In the early years, when we asked team members to list what they thought were the company's core values, responses included empathy, compassion, curiosity, caring, and humility. Many also mentioned respect, a word that we feel encompasses all those others.

Respect—for the customers we may see once in our lives and for the colleagues we labor alongside every day—is truly at the heart of our Gentle Giant HEART values. If this were the world most of us wish for, business owners wouldn't have to instruct their employees to show respect for customers—even when customers exhibit bad behavior. When our movers are confronted with boorish or hostile behavior, they are conditioned to never react with defensiveness or respond in kind. We coach them, instead, to be empathetic. They must not view the situation as a customer just being a jerk. Rather, they are coached to consider what circumstances and stressors might be affecting the customer's behavior. Then they must think hard about what can be done to improve the situation. Movers must keep in mind that they are, by necessity, getting intimate knowledge of customers' lives at a time of unavoidable vulnerability and stress. An important aspect of respect is to refrain from passing judgment.

I once moved a family where the children had chronic health conditions and were out of control. Their place was a chaotic mess, and their belongings were of little value. Their embarrassment was obvious and they were clearly humiliated by having their circumstances put on display. My helper that day was a recent hire, and all his previous jobs had been at high-end, pristine residences.

"Why did they hire us? Surely, they could have found a cheaper mover?" he asked me after we had loaded the truck.

As it happens, I had booked that move, and I understood why the customer had chosen us.

"They hired us," I told him, "because they knew they would be treated with respect."

I think a lot of companies equate respect with professionalism. The more professional your employees appear—courteous, competent, punctual—the more customers trust them. The Giants certainly conduct themselves professionally. (Our employees wear uniforms. Upon arrival, all crew members individually greet the customer.) Courtesy and professionalism can be baked into the kind of script often provided to service workers to ensure consistency of standards. But *behaving* respectfully, while essential, can be superficial. Respect—*real* respect—goes deeper. For Gentle Giants, who often meet people when they are stressed, true respect means striving to see things from the customers' point of view. That is what we want the foundation of every interaction to be.

Our crews must make it clear to the customer that this is not just another job for them. The customer is the expert in what is being moved, and why it is being moved, and how this move fits into her life story. Our movers set themselves to learn from this expert. They take in the vibes as they choreograph each unique moving experience. Great customer-service interactions, like almost all relationships, are built on conversations. So, our movers ask questions. "What are some of the most important pieces to you?" "Where did you get this fantastic painting?" Or they might elicit information with a simple statement. "This is a beautiful home. You must be sorry to leave it." And then they listen closely and attentively.

There is so much written about how important it is for leaders to listen. All of that is absolutely correct. But, in many companies, leaders don't spend nearly enough time teaching frontline people to listen. (Gentle Giant offers employees a course in listening.) Learning to listen helps develop emotional intelligence. And with emotional intelligence comes the insight and sensitivity to understand what the customer needs from them at that moment.

I am firmly aligned with those who believe that empathy can be learned. Once learned, it can become ingrained. Recently, a crew from our Beverly office was doing a move for a noticeably large customer. When she sat down on a bench that had just been unloaded from the truck, it broke beneath her. Immediately, one of our movers ran over and helped her up. Without a second thought, he grabbed the bench, turned it over and said, "I'm not surprised. It's a manufacturing defect!" This simple act of kindness saved the customer from embarrassment.

Due to a miscommunication, our crew arrived late to a move. When the customer opened the door, she was already screaming. While he packed and loaded the first floor, the crew chief, Chris Petrigno, engaged in conversation with her. Over the course of a few hours, the customer slowly opened up to him. He learned she was a recent widow, leaving her home of 50 years. Through patient listening, Chris had been able to provide a sympathetic ear in her time of unbearable stress and loss.

This lady had a vintage sign advertising Moxie soda hung in her kitchen. Wanting to deepen the connection he was forging with her, Chris told her that, as a child, he had started drinking Moxie with his grandfather. He still drank the stuff (bitter aftertaste notwithstanding) because of that sentimental association. As Chris was unwrapping the Moxie sign in her new home, the woman told him to keep it. It was her gift to him. It hangs in his kitchen to this day, and he named his dog Moxie.

We spend a lot of time coaching new movers on the skill of connecting with customers, but in Chris' case, he came to us with an innate ability to do so. I remember another Gentle Giant, Ben Swanson, who was also a natural when it came to making connections with customers. On Ben's first job as a crew chief, I went with him for backup. We walked into a pristine home which our customer, Celia, had furnished with an impressive array of fine antiques. She was in a state of high anxiety, the result of some brutal experience with previous movers. Ben was surprised to see a beautiful grandfather clock that had not been mentioned to our Sales Department. "Don't worry," she said, "the people I bought it from are coming to prepare it."

However, those clock-moving people called to say they were delayed until late afternoon. Realizing Celia would have to rely on us to handle the clock, Ben assured her that we could. Needing reassurance, Celia asked him to show her exactly how he would prepare it. Ben set to work right away to gain her confidence and help her relax. He walked over to the clock and examined it carefully, remarking on the make. He was actually not yet qualified to be in charge of moving a tall case clock. Then he uttered words that were magic to Celia, "Wow," he said, "This is a beautiful clock, probably the nicest I've seen since I've been in the business."

With that, you could see all the anxiety leave the customer and observe her sense of relief. She sure had hired someone who appreciated her clock. Then he said, "Why don't I have Larry go over everything with you. He is a real expert." I could see that she was totally impressed that I knew more about grandfather clocks than Ben.

It is not every day that you learn from an employee. I knew the value of showing customers my appreciation of their prized possessions, but I don't think I would have had the presence of mind to do what Ben did. What I learned was that, when possible, showing appreciation for a cherished possession can be the first step toward allaying any concerns about moving it.

A couple of hours later, Celia asked me if Ben had a girlfriend. Her daughter had just broken up with someone she thought was a real jerk, and she was hoping Ben would go on a blind date with her. He did, but nothing came of it. But just think, Ben brought a customer around from worrying that he might damage her precious possessions to considering bringing him into the family. Ben just retired from a successful career as an executive for U.P.S.

One day, a job took a very bad turn, and I am so proud of how the crew on that particular move responded. The customer was relocating to a beautiful condo in Boston's Back Bay neighborhood, where she expected her New York-based fiancée would soon join her. Our people had just started the job when the fiancée called and, out of the blue, ended the relationship. The crew had seen the customer happy and excited. Suddenly, the ground caved in beneath her. She was so upset that she was shaking and could not direct the crew. Our movers worried she might harm herself.

Remember some of the proposed core values that we ultimately rolled into Respect. Compassion. Empathy. Caring. Our team understood that, in that moment, the customer was in crisis and needed more than just a moving job. The crew chief called our Director of Safety, John Zimmer, who drove over immediately. He supported her as she sobbed, and they decided together that she should go to Massachusetts General Hospital. He drove her there and he stayed with her.

Winning Over the Resistant Customer

We coach our people never to throw in the towel. If the customer isn't happy, you still might be able to win them over. Right up until the invoice is presented and you're saying goodbye, there's a chance to turn things around. Steve Tracy, a quintessential enthusiastic crew chief and his crew were once met by a customer spewing venom. Steve, seeking to follow his training and engage with her, said: "You don't like us very much now, do you?" When she agreed with him, he said: "That's all right. You don't have to like us now. But when this job is over, you will be leaping in the air shouting, 'I love the Giants!'"

The customer gave Steve a bewildered look. But his words energized the rest of the crew. They couldn't believe he'd said that to her. As a result, our people ran their legs off and blew that job out much faster than anyone would have thought possible. At the end, as they were running in the last boxes, Steve said to her, "Come on now! Give us a jump!" And she did it! She gave a little jump and said, "I love the Giants!"

On one move, in Washington D.C., the customer was unrelentingly sour throughout. The crew chief tried every technique he knew to win her over. No luck. As he was driving away, he recalled that he had "thank-you" cards in the truck, which we encourage movers to send to customers who have been unusually nice. That is one of those small opportunities for connection described above.

The crew chief pulled over, took out a card, and wrote, "Even though I feel we failed to meet your expectations, it was a pleasure working with you." He drove back, knocked on the door, and handed the customer the card. She read it, teared up, reached out and hugged him.

You hear from business owners all the time that some customers can't be satisfied. On rare occasions, that might be true. But you must remember that people aren't just difficult to be difficult. If they are unhappy, and even if it appears to be for illogical reasons, our crews are trained to strive to understand things from the customer's point of view. If you're truly committed, as we are, to winning the customer's heart, you'll find a way to work things out.

When the crew is unable to resolve a complaint, we have an amazing quality control team led by Joe Ingaharro. Between our movers and Joe's people, fewer than a dozen of the more than 18,000 shipments we handle per year present issues that are not amicably resolved in a reasonable time frame. At some companies, those seemingly hopeless cases might be pushed to the farthest back burner. At Gentle Giant, they are escalated to top priority.

Tom O'Gorman has been our CEO since I stepped back from that role in 2020, so now these difficult cases are his to resolve. But for many decades before Tom succeeded me, I was the one who dealt with these top-priority, recalcitrant problems. Here is how I dealt with them: First, I would ask the disgruntled customer to choose a day when she could take a call between 5:30 PM and 6:00 PM. At the appointed time, I would call her while pulling out of the parking lot in my car, with the phone on speaker.

As I drove, I would let the customer talk. Whenever they paused to catch their breath, I would ask a clarifying question. When they seemed to be running out of steam, I would ask more questions. When the customer was finally tapped out, I wanted to make sure I understood their point of view correctly. Then, I would repeat their arguments back to them. Most customers would agree with my summary. A few would say, "No, no, no. You've got it all wrong!" Then they'd start in on it again, as if rehearsing a stage play. On those nights, my dinner had a date with the microwave.

If a person is difficult like that, chances are they've given grief to others as well. They expect to be met with impatience and exasperation: not invited to speak their piece. Nor are they accustomed to anyone genuinely listening. When someone in a business listens and cares—especially when that someone is the owner or CEO—then they are more likely to listen back. That simple exchange of courtesy and respect is remarkably effective. Although it has often cost us money, over the years I've resolved at least 90% of these seemingly intractable conflicts. Of course, resolutions cannot always be in our favor. Almost always, however, my respectful listening and transparent, good-faith efforts at resolution have had a positive impact.

Some customers won't tell you to your face they're unhappy. We had done a lot of work for one woman who had always liked the crews, until we moved her mother. At the new home, we did everything according to her mother's instructions. After we left, the daughter visited and became irate because, personally, she would have arranged things differently. I guarantee that if the daughter had been there during the move, everything would have been fine.

Another regular customer, who happened to work with this woman, called to tell me she was trashing us around the office. We did all we could to get her to discuss the situation, but with no luck. Still, I persisted and eventually coaxed her to meet with me in person. I presented her with an apology and a beautiful bouquet. I suspected that this woman was avoiding us because she did not want to have to defend what she had been saying about us. But I didn't rehash the details. I simply said I was sorry. It restored a positive connection. The bad-mouthing ceased.

Helping Customers Teach Us

Gathering customer feedback is essential to maintaining the highest standards of service. We emphasize the importance of letting us know when something goes awry. So much of a company's reputation depends on how it responds when something goes wrong. When customers see how we step up to address the problem, it often leaves them more impressed than if a job went perfectly. So, whether they tell us directly or leave a review online, it's a win-win, provided we can identify the reviewer.

We survey customers after every job. But getting useful feedback often requires a proactive approach. Some customers, as long as they are generally satisfied, automatically give us top marks across the board. That's fine for more straightforward services such as Uber. But we are seeking more granular information so that we can learn as much as possible from each survey response. Ideally, our crew chiefs will have the chance to hang around for a few minutes after a move to talk with the customer. That's something I used to do when I could. My teammates were often tired and hungry (and no doubt so was I). But it is in those conversations that you learn what could have gone better. You must ask the question, though. You must make the customer believe you genuinely want criticism. Not just, "I hope you liked our work and don't forget to rate us."

We used to ask people to rate us on a 10-point scale. We almost always got 10s or 9s. That made us feel grand. But we worried about the pitfall of complacency. It's hard to motivate employees to improve when everyone is telling them they're already perfect. So, we switched to a 15-point scale, where 13, 14, and 15 were considered excellent. That way, people could give us lower scores without feeling they were being too critical. With that scale, customers give you more granular information. They also see that you really want this information. That may be the most resonant thing customers take away from the encounter that the experience mattered as much to you as it did to them. Some people, however, are so conflict-adverse, or perhaps so nice, they will not report the slightest dissatisfaction. To address this, we do everything we can to emphasize our determination to redress any complaints or concerns.

Managing the Online Profile

Rating services, if structured with integrity and common sense, can provide a needed public service. In the mid-nineties, a wonderful company called Angie's List popped up. Their product was a list of companies that could help people find good service. People paid a modest annual fee to access lists of top-rated companies. Subscribers submitted ratings of completed jobs. This was a perfect system, and we were proud to win many Angie's Super Service awards.

Over time, other companies entered the rating service business. Now, suddenly, the rating information was being offered for free. Where do these "no subscription" companies get their revenue? From the companies that are being rated, of course! The companies that are being rated supply advertising revenue to the company doing the rating! Once the option to get rating information for free existed, many fewer were willing to pay the modest fees. Angie's List was sold and the new owners got rid of the annual fee and adopted the funding model used by Yelp and other competitors. It should be blatantly obvious (but unfortunately, it is not obvious to the public) that reviews should not be considered reliable when the review site is pressuring those being rated for revenue. I am convinced that if Angie's List had hung in there, the public would have eventually realized the immense value of consistently reliable reviews from a source that charged a modest fee. In that system, reviews can only be written by certified members.

I first heard of Yelp when I was told that a 1-star review had been posted. Based on the review, I identified the job and circled back with the crew chief. He explained that the customer had insisted on moving everything in his fully furnished apartment into his fiancé's fully furnished apartment. There simply was not enough room for both sets of furniture. The customer became irate at the suggestion that some of his belongings might have to go into storage. Therefore, the crew had no option but to cram all the customers' belongings, including a huge armoire, into the fiancé's five-room apartment. So that explained the posted complaints about boxes piled on top of furniture and an armoire partially blocking a passageway.

After work, I went to the customer's address. He was not home yet so I waited for him. While I waited, I went online and discovered that this customer was a compulsive online reviewer of many different types of services, Gentle Giant being only one of many recent targets. I noticed he had given a very poor review of an auto body shop, which I knew was excellent. An acquittance of mine ran it and I called him. My call was the first time he had heard of Yelp. I invited him to join me as I waited. In his thick Polish accent, this nice guy implored me to "please take some deep breaths and drive away. Something bad is going to happen."

But I had the Giant HEART playbook. When the customer arrived, we made a good connection, and I went over his complaints. Even though his issues were ridiculous, we took care of them. He changed his review to a 5-star and promised me he would not hand out any more low ratings until he had given the object of his ire a chance to make things right.

The internet can be a powerful and insidious destructive force. Let's start with how information gets amassed. Everybody has the power to broadcast any perceived grievance worldwide. Some people do so without providing any feedback to the service provider, which could result in appropriate redress. For example, I was visiting a friend at his home when his son came in after having eaten at a local restaurant. He told us that, because the soup had not been hot enough for him, he had left them a 1-star review on Yelp. His father asked if he had allowed the restaurant to serve him hotter soup. The son had not complained at all. He had just whipped out his phone and posted a bad review!.

"If you had let them know about the soup and they did nothing about it, then they would deserve 1 star, but launching an attack on the livelihood of those restaurant workers makes no sense."

"Oh, Dad, you are just so old school," replied the callow son.

In this environment, where a single individual can unfairly impact a reputation, we at Gentle Giant, of course, pay close attention to online reviews. Almost all our reviews are 5-star. We focus down hard on the very few bad reviews. Because moving is a highly customized service, if one of these rare poor reviews was posted by an actual customer, we are most often able to identify the customer who posted it. In such cases, we reach out to resolve any complaint. At that point, the reviewer changes their rating to 4 or 5 stars.

For most of the poor reviews, by cross-checking the information in the post against our roster of moves, we can conclude with high confidence that it is a fake review. (Fake reviews are a common occurrence in the wild-wild hostile world of online reviews. Perhaps you can guess at some who might post fake reviews and the motivations for doing so.) Take my word for it. Trying to get those fake reviews taken down is a nightmare and requires a massive expenditure of resources—resources that, in our view, are better spent on taking care of actual customers.

In the few cases where we are neither able to identify an actual customer nor able to conclude with confidence that the review is fake, I find the frustration insufferable. I am mystified as to why a customer would not inform us of their dissatisfaction. We make our commitment to their satisfaction abundantly clear. Those who post reviews online without prior communication with the service provider act neither in their own interests nor in the public's interests. They are certainly acting against the interests of service industry economies. Such people ignore the deep and unfair impact of their sneaky behavior on hard-working, well-intentioned service people.

And what happens to the information once it is fed into Yelp? Most people do not understand that the information on Yelp gets "filtered" by algorithms. One of these filters is designed to remove fake reviews. One of the criterion for removing fake reviews is excessive gushing. When in a charitable mood, I can force myself to perceive the comic absurdity of this situation. But most days, I just regard Yelp's underlying algorithms as infuriating. They justify this automatic filtering by the need to guard against reviews they suspect were posted by businesses themselves. I discovered this years ago while trying to understand the disconnect between what our customers said they had posted and what was displayed on the website. I was told that our reviews were over-the-top and therefore deemed likely fake.

Ever since then, we celebrate any 5-star review a customer informs us must have been filtered out as a badge of honor. Other business owners have told me that advertising on Yelp would serve us well in this situation. Yelp, of course, denies any connection between its revenue stream and its filtering algorithms. And I guess we all must take their word for that. (I assure you they do not get any revenue from us.) It is worth noting, however, that there are companies one-tenth our size that have ten times as many Yelp reviews. Turns out, that bizarre circumstance can be easily explained. Some companies offer discounts in exchange for a 5-star Yelp review.

For those of us in service industries committed to addressing customer issues, rating services that rely on advertising from those companies pose a clear and present danger. There are no checks on what is being fed in and by whom. There is very little understanding of, or transparency about, what is done with the information once it is fed in. For example, if someone seeks an online review of Gentle Giant, they could instead be bombarded with ads from the site's sponsors. My advice to readers is to ignore Yelp and others with similar business models. If you want to review a business or service, use Google. We are proud to have a close to 5-star rating on Google. Every Friday we share the best comments with the whole team. Our people truly do go above-and-beyond to provide delight, and we want to make sure they can hear the validation coming from the customers they've served.

CHAPTER SIX

A Culture of Teamwork – Tactics and Strategies

On Jay Brooks' second day on the job, he went sockless, and his feet chaffed. Feeling embarrassed for having made this stupid mistake, he did not let his crewmates know about his predicament. He worked without complaint, and by the end of the day, his feet were bleeding. When he called to explain he could not work the next day, I told him not to worry and gave him advice on caring for his feet.

Jay's next job was a big commercial move in a tall building. To minimize the amount of walking he would have to do, I put him in charge of loading the elevator. But when Jay turned the key in the freight elevator's lock, it snapped off. His heart sank. He expected his teammates to blame him and be angry with him. They were facing into a tall building where they could no longer use the elevator. But the opposite happened. His team responded with reassurance and support. Within an hour, a dozen movers showed up at the site. They hauled all the boxes and furniture up the many flights of stairs. Not a word of recrimination was spoken.

When Jay had come to work that day, he had been thinking of quitting. It was all just too hard. By day's end, he had seen how supportive, generous, and resourceful the Gentle Giant moving crews are. He had experienced firsthand our profound all-for-one, one-for-all culture. He wanted to be part of our team environment—and for the next 33 years, that is exactly what he has chosen to be. He has a core understanding of what it means for a crew to stick together and support one another. A problem for one is a problem to be solved by all.

A Culture of Teamwork

When I set out as an entrepreneur in the 1980s, corporate culture was emerging as an important concept in academia, but the term was not yet widespread within corporations. Today, the laser focus of many business leaders is on defining a workplace culture that informs and guides company values and priorities.

Seeking to foster a strong culture is a fine aspiration. Often, however, the focus is on superficial or overly narrow concerns. Your culture won't be happy just because you allow dogs in the office and put out bagels in the morning. It won't be creative by merely placing whiteboards everywhere. If, for example, a workforce of intrinsic unflinching toughness is your goal, a boot-camp-like culture might seem like a good idea. And perhaps that might work in the short term. But eventually, what you will have selected are the people who are willing to adapt to a boot camp environment, not those who live by an intrinsic code of toughness and grit.

In my opinion, it is the founder's most profound duty to foster a workplace culture grounded in a clear set of values and goals. From the beginning, the culture I have sought to foster has been one centered on teamwork. The "T" in HEART stands for teamwork. Fittingly, it comes last in our acronym; it is the culmination of all that must happen for our company to be Gentle Giant.

Throughout the years I worked on the trucks, I always partnered with the newest people. Once it became clear to me that someone had the potential to become a great mover, I would start to involve them in decisions and encourage them to take on more and more responsibility. The hope was that they would model this same behavior when they eventually became crew chiefs themselves.

Strong relationships develop on the job. The good vibes from a successful move affect the whole crew. When things go poorly, teammates bond over their shared struggle. Exhaustion can lower boundaries, making it easier to talk about feelings and joke around. And when you are out on one of those insane moves that is clearly destined to become part of the Giant lore, your teammates will be forever in your personal—as well as in the company's institutional—memory.

Physical proximity helps. Communication gets comfortable quickly when you're facing someone six feet away across a sofa that both of you are determined not to drop. Two movers, one above and one below a heavy piece of furniture, edging up a steep staircase, will develop trust more effectively than a couple of office workers on a corporate retreat falling backwards into each other's arms.

In my view, the two most crucial processes for instilling and reinforcing our culture of teamwork are: 1) switching it up (getting to where everyone is comfortable on any team, regardless of any prior experience with the team mates assigned on a given day), and 2) customizing the match between the movers assigned and the skills needed for each job.

Switching It Up

When I get a call after a job, it's often someone praising the team. Customers love watching our people interact. Their cheerful banter, the seamless way they synchronize their movements. It's like they are reading one another's minds. Repeat customers will request the same team as they had for their last move. I've had people call and ask if we can send the same team that moved them 25 years earlier.

One of the most validating calls I ever received came from a customer who taught organizational behavior and studied teams for a living. She told me that the Giants who moved her were just about the most well-oiled team she had ever encountered. She assumed they must have worked together for a long time. But Gentle Giant doesn't have set teams. In fact, we switch them up every day. On that particular move, one crew member had not done a single job with the others.

Changing things up like this is both a motivational and a preventative tactic. Every time a Giant goes out with a different mix of people, they are demonstrating what they can contribute. The more the crews mix, the more they can learn from each other. Each must maintain the crew's seamless efficiency and match the performance of their co-workers. When movers shift among teams, they can be reassured that standards are consistent. They have a sense of pride that they can measure up, even when they are paired with a Giant legendary in our lore.

Constant change also makes it easier to adapt when teams suddenly expand. At Gentle Giant, if a job goes sideways—as happened in the story that opens this chapter—then we may have to send help. That typically means some number of additional movers detailed from a nearby regional office. In those situations, there's no time for new teammates to get used to one another. The original team needs to quickly and smoothly incorporate the new additions into its workflow.

I am always gratified when movers who have never previously worked together can collaborate like old comrades. And it's not just coordinating on a physical level. I've seen Giants from different regional branches come together to solve complex problems that would leave most folks flummoxed. For example, Chris Petrigno was crew chief on a move from Boston to Pennsylvania where the customer, a pianist, was joining the Philadelphia Symphony Orchestra. He and another Massachusetts Giant drove for 6 hours to the job site, where they met up with a Philadelphia crew.

The move involved an extraordinary 9-foot concert grand piano. Numerous famous pianists had autographed it and was worth well into six figures. The customer had bought the house because it had a room perfect for practicing on this concert grand. But our movers discovered it was physically impossible to maneuver the piano around a corner and into the room. This freshly formed team began brainstorming. They came up with the idea of cutting a hole in the wall of the room adjacent to the piano's intended home. The Giants created an opening in the drywall and slid the instrument in. A few contractors were working in the house. The Giants asked if they could build a door to fill the hole. This was done expeditiously. The customer was elated.

When a crew unexpectedly needs help, the switched-up composition allows things to run smoothly with camaraderie. We had a crew that found itself with an unexpectedly daunting offload. The customer's new home was enormous and already had rooms full of heavy furniture that needed to be moved before the belongings could come in. On top of that, it was 90 degrees and humid. Morale sagged as the realization of what lay ahead sank in.

Meanwhile, back at the warehouse, movers who were done for the day were grilling steaks, kicking back, and having fun. When the overwhelmed crew members called for help, their friends didn't hesitate. Within an hour, another five or six movers were at the job site. And they brought steaks and grilled vegetables. The original crew's spirits soared. The job was finished amid great good cheer.

A lot of companies—moving companies included—like to keep team composition the same. The owners of such companies explain that when the same people work together consistently, they establish rhythms. Everyone knows each other's strengths and weaknesses, which makes task assignment easier. They say it leads to fewer mistakes. While it is true that, when your composition is static, your best teams will stay good and may even keep improving. Teams that need improvement will, in the meantime, settle into the norm of mediocrity, and there will be no strategy in place to shake them out of it. If the team's composition doesn't change, its performance won't either.

In a static team that isn't great to start with, they won't want a new addition showing them up. When you're comfortable performing at a 6, you don't want the boss to realize that 10 is within reach. And if you're a 10 kind of person on a 6 kind of team, you'll either take it down a few notches or take a hike. No one wants to carry lazy people on their backs. Switching it up ensures that all our teams are A Teams. Once, at a reception, a prominent member of the business community who had booked a job with us said to me: "You will send me your A Team, won't you." I can't blame him for asking me that annoying question, because most companies do have their A, B and C teams.

I had an early experience with norms when I was a student at Northeastern, doing maintenance and repairs around campus to make some money. On my first day, I found myself on a five-member team assigned work that I could have managed alone or easily with the help of one other person. I thought it was idiotic, but I went along with the status quo. Every time I cashed my paycheck, I felt like I was pulling off a minor heist.

One morning, I woke up with strep and called in sick. The next week, when I collected my check, I saw I had been paid for the missed day. I spoke to the person who had taken my call and told him about the mistake. "Don't worry about it," he said. "I punched you in and out. I took care of you." My stomach turned as I realized I had unwillingly been made a part of a (small) criminal conspiracy.

A couple of weeks later, at the beginning of the day, the team captain said there was a call for me in the office. It was the guy who had punched me in. He said he didn't feel like coming to work that day. Would I mind punching him in and out? I shouldn't have done it. But I did it, and that is how easily a person can get drawn into the prevailing workplace standards. When I look back on this, I am thankful that I managed to come to my senses and realize that this was not the person that I wanted to be. The next time I saw my corrupting influence, I told him we were even, and this would never happen again.

Years later, with this episode still on my mind, I vowed a culture like that would never invade Gentle Giant. If a bad apple managed to find a home on a static team by being chummy with teammates, treating them to drinks and doing little favors, calling him out becomes difficult. It can even feel like a betrayal of a friend. Switching it up is one of the tactics we use to prevent any such workplace dilemmas. No one team can develop their own private set of norms.

A good example of how well the "switching it up" tactic sustains our culture and serves our customers occurred when two movers independently approached me about one specific crew chief who we had hired from another company. Both movers reported that when assigned as crew chief to their respective teams, the person in question had urged them to slow down. "What's your hurry?" he'd asked as they hustled through a job. These movers had never experienced this kind of talk from other crew chiefs. They recognized when someone was trying to impose non-Giant values.

Although this employee had many of the qualities we insist upon, he lacked the "hustle"—the E (enthusiasm)—in the Giant HEART values. The switching policy and its reasons are well understood and accepted within the company. In many workplace cultures, people who point out bad behavior are regarded as snitches or worse. The example above involving an experienced hire from another company highlights the strength of our workplace culture. Our movers knew that this crew chief did not belong at Gentle Giant and they acted in the interests of Gentle Giant and its customers. I have explained that we coach our people to first address concerns directly to someone's face. But in this case, it clearly made sense to go over his head. Had we not acted, the faith of our movers in our commitment to the HEART values would have been severely shaken.

Customizing Crews for Each Job

Assembling the optimal combination of people requires expertise and finesse. Each job requires close collaboration between sales, dispatchers, crew chiefs, and group leaders. We must make sure that people with the appropriate mix of experience and skills are matched to each job. At Gentle Giant, perhaps the most important first question our salespeople ask is: Why are you moving? Often, the move is related to one of life's great stresses, such as a death or a loss of autonomy due to aging. If so, the dispatcher will assign a crew chief known for ability to connect with empathy and forbearance. The match with technical aspects of the job is, of course, also vital. Does the move involve large heavy furniture with tight access or particularly fragile items? How many trucks will be needed? How long will the job take? (Hours? Days?) Does the customer live in a state of clutter or disorganization? Is Gentle Giant packing or has the customer opted to pack themselves? How many flights of stairs? Are there time restrictions on elevator use?

So, there is nothing random about the match between movers and jobs. Our commitment to ensuring that each customer gets a customized crew poses challenges for the dispatcher that outsiders cannot appreciate. For example, one of our all-time greatest crew chiefs, in terms of knowledge, work ethic, strength, problem-solving, and efficiency, did not, we all knew, pay attention to making a connection with customers. Unless the customer noticed what he was doing and initiated a conversation, he barely said a word. So, when he was sent on a residential move, the dispatcher assigned a teammate who would compensate for this deficit. Similar consideration is given to the physical requirements of each job. A 60-year-old mover is not assigned to a fourth-floor walkup. A mover who worked a bone-crushing job one day is not expected to work the same type of job the next day.

It is also important to pair less experienced people with experienced ones. As we assemble teams, keeping our need for continuous training in mind allows for continued growth and development. These growth opportunities within our team structure elevate morale and produce the next set of experienced people. Dispatchers and group leaders draw from a deep well of available information that has been accumulated starting with the Stadium run and continuing with evaluations by crew chiefs during on-the-job training. With so many factors to consider, dispatchers have very high-pressure responsibilities. Ultimately, they must: a) be aware of the reasons each team member has been chosen for a particular job, and b) be sure that each team has been constructed for optimal customer service. When it's time for movers to stretch towards leadership, we place them with crew chiefs who will guide them in that transition.

Tending to Teamwork Dynamics

Good teamwork makes a job the best in the world. Team dysfunction leads to workplace misery. We train and coach team dynamics. It is much to our advantage that most movers come to us with experience in collaborative team sports. If you feel a teammate could be better, you help them get better. And you always make sure you are doing your personal best. The fluidity of leadership, also integral to success in team sports, is foundational to our success at Gentle Giant. No one person makes all the decisions. Egos remain in check. Roles change as every member gets the chance to step up. All teammates are encouraged to showcase their strengths. On our teams, teammates feed one another energy, support, and guidance. Teammates both teach and learn from one another. Veterans encourage all crew members to contribute.

Team members should feel secure. It is particularly important in companies like ours, where most of the work is physical. Workers develop trust by visibly exercising the vigilance and caution required to keep one another safe. Our teams form bonds as they fight shoulder to shoulder through punishing ordeals. Together, they celebrate hard-won triumphs. Deep friendships are often forged. Camaraderie born from teamwork is a widely enjoyed part of our culture.

Just as we develop the soft skills that help our movers relate to their customers, we emphasize that those same skills are equally important as they interact with one another. People should be able to read their teammates' moods and emotions. They should look out for one another in high-stress situations. That means being adept at calming the stressed, motivating the demoralized, and soothing the angry. In the event of a job "blowing up," teammates should be ready to step up and figure out how they can relieve some of the crew chief's stress.

What Isaac Pulkkinen did for his crew chief, Jon Powell, is a great example of a crew member stepping up to help a crew chief. The customer had booked the job with the assurance that everything would be packed and ready to go. But no preparation had actually been done. Several additional movers had been called in as the scale of the job became clear. As the movers dashed around wrapping and boxing, the customer dithered about each decision. She led Jon through the house—which was very large—telling him what she wanted in her new home and what she wanted donated. Then, she changed her mind and repeated that process. And repeated it … and then again. By 6 PM, when it was getting dark. Jon felt like he'd fallen into a time loop from which there was no escape.

Noticing how beaten down Jon was becoming with each frustrating decision change, Isaac offered to step in to take a fresh approach with the waffling, and by now exhausted, customer. Politely but firmly, Isaac insisted that the customer agree to declare each of her decisions as "final for good." "So, that's your decision with this stuff. And that's what we're going to do with it. And we're not coming back to it. Agreed? OK, on to the next decision." As a result of Isaac's intervention, the job got done that night. Jon was impressed with Isaac's maturity and ability to step up with intelligence and empathy. Far from feeling that rank had been jumped, Jon was grateful for the much-needed rescue.

What crew chief Rob Leaver did to make one job much easier for his crew is a good example of what a team member, in this case the crew chief, did to reduce his team's workload. The move involved moving from one house on a corner to the house behind it, which faced onto a different street. The customer expected the crew to carry everything to the street and around two corners to the new home. On the day before the move, as Rob was packing up the first house, he noticed construction going on in the yards between the two houses. He realized that if everything was carried across the yards instead, the job would be greatly expedited. But the obstacle to that option was that the yard was a sea of mud due to the construction. Rob purchased materials for a plywood walkway between the houses. He had the walkway laid before the crew arrived the next day. The work was much easier for his crew, and the customer was delighted by how efficiently the job was done.

In Chapter 4, I covered feedback as our elixir of success. I believe peer-to-peer feedback and training on how to deliver it should be ingrained in workplace culture. We emphasize how important it is to our culture of teamwork. Every one of us is both a teacher and a student. We encourage kudos and offer training on when and how to address areas for improvement. Effective feedback, especially peer feedback, requires a culture of trust and a belief in teammates' best intentions. At Gentle Giant, those are characteristics of our culture of teamwork. If feedback involves polishing someone's performance, teammates are encouraged to discuss it among themselves. But if a new hire fails to meet our HEART standards or, for example, is careless about safety, then reporting this to a supervisor is required.

Gossiping or talking behind people's backs poisons effective teamwork. In an environment that includes people who lack strong core values, gossip flourishes. Talking behind people's backs violates the value of respect. We strive to make avoiding gossip easier for our employees by hiring people with strong HEART values. With these values firmly in place, coaching our employees to address issues face-to-face is a natural progression. We give them strategies for delivering feedback in ways that lead to constructive outcomes. It is also necessary to coach people on what to do when they are the recipient of gossip. There is a real danger that even the best-intentioned person will nod in agreement, thereby feeding the fire. We want them to know that they need to speak up and encourage their teammates to talk directly to the source of their criticism.

Because people with strong HEART values tend to be easily approachable, these conversations can occur with a friendly vibe. If someone is considering reporting a teammate to a manager, the respectful thing to do is give that person a heads-up. A crew member might say, "As you know, this is a non-smoking company. I've asked you not to smoke. If this keeps happening, I'm going to speak to your manager." That person is then on notice that he is being held accountable.

Personalities do sometimes clash of course. People get upset. We do not ignore such upsets because our whole system is based on everyone working with everyone else. No one can dodge their least favorite Giant. We have guidelines for dealing with conflict. We coach on smoothing out rocky relationships. We, of course, point out to employees that conflict-management skills must be applied not just when dealing with our customers but also when issues arise among teammates. Don't react while in an emotional state. Listen to the other person. Understand that people won't listen until they themselves feel they have been heard. Ask questions. Repeat back to the person what you think they've said. Be self-aware.

Crew Chief as Team Leader

At Gentle Giant, we ask crew chiefs to keep in mind that they have four roles: mover, team leader, mentor, and role model. Working with a variety of our veteran crew chiefs provides our movers with broad sampling of people filling these four roles. Our movers can learn more and the company can grow stronger.

We expect our crew chiefs to empower the team to participate in decisions. As I mentioned earlier, this was always a belief of mine, but overcoming my instinct to control was a personal challenge. Regarding this challenge, I learned a great deal from Steve Hart, one of our most legendary crew chiefs. Although he knew more about moving than anyone else, Steve would ask his teammate, "What do you think?" This approach was natural for him, and through his example, it has been modelled and firmly established at Gentle Giant.

It is true that the crew chief likely has more experience than other movers on the team. But with no two jobs the same, challenges without an obvious path forward can arise. It's commonplace for a crew chief to follow the Steve Hart approach and ask a teammate: "What do you think we should do here?" Of course, a recent hire might at first react like a deer in the headlights but will soon become comfortable thinking things through and contributing to solutions. This is the routine experience in our culture of teamwork. Crew chiefs listen and gain the advantage of diverse inputs. For rising crew chiefs as they transition into the role and become comfortable with shared decision making, this pervasive culture of collaborative leadership is a great advantage. However, all our movers understand that final responsibility must rest with the crew chief. In crises, the crew chief must take control and make decisions quickly.

Cementing Field-Office Bonds

We believe that creating opportunities for people to get to know each other is vitally important. Movers rotate through the office. Office workers will often shadow our teams on moves. Fostering relationships through formal and informal gatherings helps us cement the bonds between departments. We celebrate our Gentle Giant culture through cookouts, parties with children's games, award banquets, and sports teams with office/field mix.

We believe that great relationships between the people in the field and those in the office lead to superior customer experience. The people in the field might be delivering great customer service. The people in the office might be performing at the highest level. In the absence of strong relationships between fields and the office, the company will not thrive. Recognizing the importance of trusting, cordial relationships between field and office staff, we have focused on coaching for effective, respectful communication. Inter-departmental training sessions are run for this purpose. Our expectations are made clear—the teamwork culture must encircle all of us.

Imagine, for example, a scenario where a customer says to a mover: "Your salesperson low-balled the job." There are two ways the mover might reply. The first reply might be a common one in some companies, but it is a reply that no Gentle Giant should ever give: "Yes, that person can low-ball." If a reply like this were given, the mover would have diverted the customer's dissatisfaction towards another of our employees and preserved his own chances of a tip. The salesperson would have been thrown under the bus, without any opportunity to understand and learn from any valid complaint the customer might have. The customer would stay angry and disappointed, and likely post a bad review. The company would have been hurt, both by leaving a dissatisfied customer and by a trust breach between the salesperson and the mover.

The second reply is the one that a Gentle Giant will give, and it will be the truthful one: "I am so sorry. I work closely with that salesperson, and rarely has there been an issue." Then he will talk with the customer to understand things from that perspective. If he feels that the customer has a point, he will circle back with the salesperson later to share any lessons learned. If circling back with the customer is appropriate, that will also be done.

At Gentle Giant, with ingrained HEART values, our crews know they must be completely transparent with the customer and that they have the trust of our Quality Control dept. This is vitally important to our company's success. QC can proceed with resolutions having full confidence that they have the facts. Here, as everywhere, ingrained HEART values serve us well.

In the moving industry, claims are often outsourced. And even when companies handle claims themselves, they deal directly with the claimant and usually leave the crew chief (often a contractor) out of the conversation. To us, that is the opposite of teamwork. We recognize the importance of fostering relationships between the field and the office. When a customer raises a question or complaint, field and office teams work together to identify the causes and develop solutions. Sales relies on field workers for feedback. Field workers inform the salesperson when an estimate is off. Us-against-them leads to a formula for failure. One-for-all leads to success.

CHAPTER SEVEN

Taking New Markets The Gentle Giant Way

Kris Walker's 2005 opening of our New York City office is a great example of how the Gentle Giant prototype can be replicated while accounting for a city's unique character. He had moved to the New York region the previous year to live close to his future wife and was coaching a rowing program for teens when we asked him to open a New York office for us. It took a few months to learn the area and develop connections by attending Chamber of Commerce events and meeting local realtors for coffee. He was doing the groundwork to build a business in a new market, doing whatever it took to open doors and get the phone ringing.

In the beginning, he was booking mostly small jobs. Because he still did not have enough work to hire full-time movers, he mirrored what I had done in my early days. Every time a job was booked, he would reach out to one of his robust relations or his rowing and mountain-climbing friends until he found someone who could commit that day. He eventually had a great collection of first-class people who were trained and rearing to go if they could shake free when he needed them. A few months after launch, he noticed a huge, expensive house on the market in Westchester. An entrepreneurial fellow, Kris contacted the realtor and asked to be alerted when it sold. When it did, he reached out to the couple who had owned it: married doctors who were empty-nesting and moving to a smaller place. He set up a meeting and pitched them hard on the Giants.

So, there was Kris with this massive job that could potentially lead to many others. After an inventory, he realized he'd need four trucks and a crew of at least ten people, including drivers. But he'd made the sale. At that point, he had just one truck, on a long-term lease. He had to knock it out of the park. Ordinarily, Gentle Giant would be there 24/7 to send in the cavalry and supply the resources needed for a situation like this. However, with a brand-new office, although Kris might have been on his own, he was more than ready. He wasn't going to lose this opportunity; he had created his own cavalry. He lined up three extra rental trucks. By then, he had hired two full-time movers and among the people he had trained were his father-in-law and the father-in-law's friend, who luckily had commercial driver's licenses. With plenty of lead time, he got on the phone and rounded up the talent needed. Every person he called was willing to arrange to be available during those crucial three days he needed them. I'm sure that had a lot to do with how well he had taken care of them when they helped him in the past.

In this way, Kris was able to muster around 10 people. The job went off without a hitch. The next week, Kris took everyone out for a celebratory dinner.

Slow But Sure, We Expand

When we reached the point where the next obvious step was to become an interstate company, I had much to think about. The big van lines provide the infrastructure for most interstate moves. As we approached the 5-million-dollar mark, several companies reached out to us about becoming van line agents. Becoming a van line agent is an attractive option for local companies because when someone in their region calls the van line for service, they speak with the local agent. With this model, the van lines win by casting their net within each local market, and the local agents win by having a steady stream of business and getting a commission. The van line sales pitch to the local moving company is: "This is a way to print money. You can't lose."

But we were not interested in partnering with a van line because, by that time, I had become knowledgeable about the interstate moving industry. The van line model is greatly dependent on casual workers. (Casual workers are not company employees and therefore are not subject to employee requirements, such as, for example, tax withholding. Neither do they receive employee benefits, such as full workers' comp insurance coverage.) Before I go any further, it's important to note that this system is perfectly legal and that many fantastic household goods independent contractors provide top-quality service. My point is that with the system reliant on casual workers, it is not possible to consistently deliver quality service.

Within the van line's network of agents, salespeople are on commission and are therefore highly incentivized to lowball estimates. This works out fine for the van lines and the agents because getting some cut of the action is better than getting none, and independent contractors do the actual moves. Those contractors then bear all the costs of labor, truck payments, repairs, fuel, insurance, road taxes and tolls, etc. In addition to this, they have to find their own movers and can only afford to pay them as casual workers. This situation can lead to poor outcomes for customers because workers are often untrained, which inevitably leads to damage and mistakes. After receiving a very professional sales pitch, the customer often must endure service from a random cast of characters. I could never ask people to place their trust in me when I do not even know who will show up to do the job.

We needed to develop a foolproof system that would provide our customers with fully trained, professional movers—Gentle Giant employees with benefits. I was determined to craft our company into a smooth-running organization that could guarantee flawless interstate work, or you're getting your money back. How could we offer guaranteed interstate service to our customers? The obvious answer was by having all the work done exclusively by Gentle Giant.

Passionate about our business, we know that what we do is truly special and hard to get right. For us, the only path forward has been, and will remain, to plant and grow new offices ourselves. This strategy will not lead us to expand as fast or as far as if we had chosen franchise or acquisition strategies. But we know what our new customers and employees will experience: Giant HEART service enveloped in a culture of teamwork.

For me, who realized early on that providing the best possible customer service meant Gentle Giant had to become a people development company, expansion has allowed us to continue being just that. Scaling nationally is our opportunity to retain some of our best employees. In New England, we have only so many manager spots available for master crew chiefs hungry to advance. It happens with some regularity that life changes pull great people away from the region. Typically, a spouse or romantic partner wants to relocate for a new job, continuing education, or family considerations. Opening a Giant office in this target location allows us to retain a top employee, which is a source of great personal satisfaction.

The most important factors in the decision to open each branch are the leader and the location. We need an entrepreneurial Giant HEART manager who started with us as a mover. If possible, we set up in a location that our employees can easily reach by bicycle or public transportation. We always keep in mind that we have a lot to offer AND a lot to learn. We know that each location presents its own brainstorming challenges and adaptation requirements.

Our expansion strategy has been multifaceted, and I see each facet as mission-critical. By strictly adhering to this strategy, we've survived in our expansion cities, including Charlotte, where the Great Recession of 2008 hit at the end of our second year there. First, we staff each new branch exclusively with our own people. We expand in stepwise progression. We started with satellite offices in New England. We now have 13 satellite branches in the New England region and operate branches in 11 other states. With the opening of each branch, the Gentle Giant Model has been replicated. 1) Start with one Giant who possesses the necessary attributes, 2) Use a hiring process that identifies "**SHOULD**-do-the-job" people, 3) Adhere to the Gentle Giant HEART values, 4) The job is not done until the customer is happy, 5) Let word-of-mouth be the fundamental marketing strategy.

Our first foray into markets outside Massachusetts were Rhode Island and New Hampshire. Those states were close enough to headquarters that our Boston managers were available to support and guide. Also, team members could switch locations, providing maximum scheduling flexibility. It was all very convenient. A key and unusual facet of our expansion strategy is that we open new branches only if we can do so without taking a loan. We expect to lose money in the beginning—sometimes a lot of money. We start out keeping overhead as low as possible. Another key and perhaps unusual facet of our strategy: we expect and accept that, at first, we will not be able to charge the premium price for a premium service we command in New England. In many parts of the country, customers still view moving as an uncomplicated commodity, just as they did in Boston before I made it my mission to change that perception.

We now have more than enough experience to be confident that once word spreads, customers will realize that the service Gentle Giant provides is worth more than we charge. So, we start with price shoppers and convert them into customers for life. We do not let a glut of competition in a particular market deter us. We instead consider the quality of the competition. Often, you'll find there are a lot of awful moving companies, especially in states with little regulation. It may seem that consumers in those places have plenty of choices, when, in fact, they don't have the choice of great service.

While strictly adhering to the key elements of our expansion strategy, we aim to maintain as much operational flexibility as the situation requires. Expansion might mean operating out of a self-storage facility or running things from the manager's home office. Sometimes, we might rent warehouse space from a local company with excess capacity. We can plan on initial staffing of just two or three people. We can rely, as I did when I started out, on rental or long-term leases from companies like Ryder and Penske.

People who build successful local businesses have two other options when deciding whether and how to expand—franchising and acquisition. Gentle Giant could have chosen either of these two options. I have often been approached by people who want to help us franchise our brand. I am not against franchising in general, but for franchising to be successful, there must be across-the-board consistency. Customers who use us in multiple locations tell us that their experiences have been remarkably consistent. I know we can deliver that consistency only because all our offices are run by managers who have come up through our system. They are steeped in the Giant HEART culture. Going forward, a strategy of acquisition might also have appeared to be an option. But our goal is to replicate something amazing, and buying existing businesses would kill our culture through dissonance, dilution, or both.

The StartUp Manager

When setting up a new branch, our VP of operations, Pat Inman, first identifies the manager to lead it. This person has always come up through the Gentle Giant ranks as a mover. Our startup managers must be entrepreneurial. While we do encourage our people to be enterprising, there is no set playbook for developing the skills of an entrepreneur. We always keep our eyes peeled for indications of an innate entrepreneurial spirit. Some very entrepreneurial people have gravitated toward Gentle Giant over the years. Some employees have left to launch their own businesses. When Tom O'Gorman, now our CEO, joined at the entry level in 1994, his plan was to start his own business someday. Luckily, for us, building Gentle Giant with us has fulfilled all his entrepreneurial yearnings.

We need our startup managers to be self-starting, initiative-taking. We want them to be comfortable navigating different client communities and naturally inclined to strike up conversations at the gym or in line at a ticket window. As we prepare crew chiefs to manage new locations, they are assigned to run larger and larger jobs, shadow members of the sales team, and take training with each of our departments (e.g., finance, quality assurance, and HR). Often, they do a stint at a new office that launched a year or two previously.

The challenge of word-of-mouth marketing is getting those first mouths to talk. That's why the entrepreneurial spirit is so important. Connecting with customers during a job is covered in Gentle Giant 101. Our delighted customers are wonderful evangelists. But their ability to spread the good word is limited to their social and professional circles. Realtors, by contrast, talk to people acquiring and selling homes every day and routinely recommend movers, as do mortgage brokers, home inspectors, and other related providers. Making inroads into that community is high on the "to do" list for a new branch manager.

Andrew Rozzi, who opened our Philadelphia office in 2015, booked a realtor as one of his first jobs. Just think about what that tells you about Andrew. For one of his first jobs, he managed to book a realtor! What a coup it was to book a professional who routinely works closely with people in the process of moving, and who therefore must already know a lot about the established movers in the area. Just imagine how persuasive Andrew must have been. His work impressed this realtor so much that her recommendations to clients gave his branch a strong start. Then he amplified that boost by taking her entire team out to lunch and delivering a well-prepared sales pitch. Ten years later, that real estate company continues to refer clients to us. Some of those agents have moved on to other employers, providing Gentle Giant with advocates in multiple agencies across the region.

With Andrew's encouragement, his crew chiefs often ask their happy customers for permission to call their realtors. Those calls broadly widen the circle of referral possibilities. Andrew has also successfully reached audiences at associations of realtors and professional organizers. (Organizers are decluttering experts who sometimes will optimize both ends of a move.) When he gets the chance, he'll drop by the many large apartment buildings that crowd Philly's Center City, leaving company brochures with concierges or security staff. Apartment residents often seek references from the folks in the lobby when looking for services like moving, cleaning, or home repairs. It's an easy and inexpensive form of marketing.

A National Team of "SHOULD-DO-THE-JOB" People

In each new market, Gentle Giant employees must exhibit the same energy, endurance, teamwork, and good humor that has become our trademark. Our practice of hiring athletes and relying heavily on recommendations from current and former movers has enabled us to sustain our culture of excellence. We have now reached the point where, in new locations, we often reap the benefits of our reputation as a great employer. Certain cities—particularly those with vibrant rowing scenes such as Philadelphia and Seattle—have, over the years, attracted a diaspora of rowers who know all about Gentle Giant. They spread the word among student athletes and athletes in general.

Giant veterans have been generous about connecting new branch managers to local talent. A onetime Giant who trained in San

Francisco for the national women's rugby team helped our manager there recruit several other players. During our first few years in Philly, an introduction by a former Giant to the rowing coach at Temple University yielded much of the workforce. Other connections there came through former Giants who had become athletes or coaches working at the men's and women's clubs on that city's famous Boathouse Row.

Regardless of the new host city's sports tradition, some version of the Harvard Stadium tryout tradition has taken root. New York City was the first location outside New England. Our manager, Kris Walker, did not have connections with local school athletic departments. He resorted to doing something we never had to do before. He put an ad in the newspaper. He had the good sense to specify that we were looking for people with athletic backgrounds. This produced a critical mass of promising candidates. In the interviews, he carefully observed people's reactions when he described our high demands and aspirations. Finally, to test candidates' readiness for the hard work, he took them out to run the stadium stairs at Fordham University or to do sprints around a nearby track. Those who loved it turned into Giants.

Charlotte, NC is not a rowing town, but Jon Vogel, the start-up manager there, used ingenuity to develop the Stadium-like CrossFit challenge. One of his early hires was a CrossFit fanatic. Soon, other movers were practicing those high-intensity workouts in the warehouse. After a few months, they acquired a weight set, then a monster-truck tire, and two super-thick 30-foot-long ropes. Eventually, the branch created a whole gym. During his recruiting efforts, Jon, who had attended school in Australia, enlisted two Aussi rower friends.

The three of them joined the city's Gaelic Football team, a sport very similar to Aussi-rules football, and excelled at it. This is a high-intensity, aerobic sport that requires strength and agility. Together, the three began recruiting from among their new friends and teammates. Jon was able to hire a few key people who thrived on the Giant way of working. They, in turn, recruited others. A referral network was born. Students from local universities were invited to join the Gaelic group. Once those students became members, the Giants broached the idea of becoming movers. Recruiting teammates created greater cohesion and stronger bonds.

By the second summer, Charlotte had more than 20 top movers, including some from the University of North Carolina at Charlotte's rugby and soccer teams. Now, recruits in Charlotte participate in an intense CrossFit challenge. At all hours of the day veterans and new hires can be found doing deadlifts, jumps, and swings together.

Our manager in Brooklyn is installing a similar CrossFit challenge gym. In Seattle the candidates run a 7K trail from our warehouse down to the ocean and back. In San Francisco, candidates run intense intervals up the dunes at Thornton Beach on the Pacific Coast side of the city. In Fort Lauderdale.... what else?... a beach run! In Washington, D.C., they run from the Potomac Boat Club to the Arlington Memorial Bridge, across the Potomac, and circle back north to the Francis Scott Key Bridge. This bridge crosses the Potomac to Georgetown, where they finish with 10 trips up those iconic steps featured in *The Exorcist*.

New Locations, Customized Solution

We started our expansion efforts well aware of the necessity of operational and logistical flexibility as we adapted to each unique location. For example, Andrew Rozzi, our Philadelphia Branch Manager, operated for years before we had our own brick-and-mortar location, which was by any measure a major logistical adaptation. In New York City, the mix of office and warehouse space we needed was so expensive that our manager, Kris Walker, had to start out using a gravel parking lot in Yonkers. He did not even have a loading dock.

Kris also discovered that in Manhattan, rather than parking in front of buildings, movers must load and unload from rear alleys. Opportunities to impress are reduced because the work is not visible to passers-by and because building staff often retain operational oversight. Kris responded by focusing on a few buildings in several neighborhoods with the desired customer demographics. Occasionally, he'd underprice a job just to get such a booking. By working consistently in the same buildings, the Giants became well known and trusted by building staff. And of course, this led them to recommend us both to the residents of those buildings and to friends of theirs who staffed other buildings. The elevator operators in New York City buildings can be well connected. Kris's crews endeared themselves by being on time, making way for others to use the elevators, and ensuring that the operators could take off for their own lunchbreaks. Impressed, the operators talked up the Giants to residents—providing another source for our expanding word-of-mouth referral network.

Kris came up against some ethically questionable practices. Real estate agents are positioned to recommend us to clients at the very time they need our services. Sometimes, the agents invite us to their conferences, and at these, we have great opportunities to make new connections. But some agents in New York wanted kickbacks in return for referrals. Recall that in Chapter 2, where I detail the policies Rooty and I laid out as we were deciding what kind of business we wanted to build, fifth among the six policies listed is: "We would nurture relationships with honorable real estate agents and would not give kickbacks for referrals". This is just one of many clear examples of how Giant HEART values, combined with a focus on soft skills and ethical behavior, have ensured that each expansion creates a replica of the original. I am disgusted when realtors take kickbacks. Putting myself in the shoes of a customer, it would sicken me to learn I'd taken a recommendation from someone getting paid to give it to me. We give these unethical people a wide berth. Fortunately for both Gentle

Giant and people who need moving services, there are plenty of good realtors who recommend movers based solely on their clients' experiences.

Most people these days begin searching for any type of service online. We pay close attention to our online presence, but we still rely primarily on word-of-mouth and the outreach of our entrepreneurial Giants. We know our message is always more potent when delivered in person. It turns out that one of the most effective ways to greatly elevate our profile and reputation is to provide services to non-profits. We get our name in front of lots of potential clients in one fell swoop. When we sponsor major local events, such as festivals, parades, and races, people associate us with something that is personally important to them. Such events offer opportunities to bond with a community while providing something of true value. At such events, our crews are all over the place in their distinctive uniforms, showing off their physical prowess and engaging in spontaneous conversations.

One good example of this type of community bonding is the close relationship Gentle Giant built with Windermere Real Estate, a large, prestigious firm on the West Coast. Every year, that company sponsors the Windemere Cup, an internationally competitive regatta hosted by the famous University of Washington rowing team. (A 2023 movie directed by George Clooney called *The Boys in the Boat* recounts its exploits during the 1936 Berlin Olympics.) Soon after we launched in Seattle, Windermere, which was aware of our connection to rowing, invited Gentle Giant to help finance and provide moving services for the regatta. It's a wonderful networking opportunity because real estate agents attend in droves. I've flown out for the Cup myself, in part because I knew I would enjoy rubbing shoulders there.

We reap the benefits of being able to tap into the family connections in a new location when one of our entrepreneurial Giants request a transfer "back home". When managers, their partners, or spouses have friends or extended family in the new market, those existing relationships grow into larger networks. They eventually yield both jobs and workers. In fact, I often factor in family connections when deciding who best to open a branch office for us. Charlotte is a great example. When Jon Vogel moved to Charlotte to be with his future wife Jessie, we had the perfect person to open an office for us. Jessie's family provided some of Gentle Giant's first big jobs in that market. We did one huge move—two tractor trailers' worth—for Providence Day School, a prestigious college-prep institution where Jon's new mother-in-law was employed. His new father-in-law ran BrewFest, the very popular charitable event of Carolina BrewMasters Homebrew Club. John's team provided BrewFest with moving and logistics. And the Giants of Charlotte didn't just join the Chamber of Commerce—they moved it to new headquarters. Our crew worked until 2 AM for each of the two days on that job. That certainly helped raise our profile with commercial customers.

Keeping the Giant Ties Strong

As we expand, we actively promote maintaining strong bonds among our regional offices. Once embedded in their branch, we fly Giants to Boston to spend time at headquarters to truly absorb our culture. Here, they do classroom work and receive specialized training, mostly in technical, city-centric skills such as hoisting heavy objects from decks and balconies. As with all Gentle Giant development, most of their training takes place on our regional trucks. Our policy of switching up teammates pays off, as our movers from all over the country meld seamlessly into New England crews formed fresh each day.

These visits between branches run both ways. It's not enough for far-flung Giants to see their company's leaders in our domain. We also need to see them in theirs. Those national locations are part of us—contributors not just to our revenue but also to our morale, our reputation, and our sense of who we are. We need to experience what it means to be a Giant in Phoenix, Seattle, and San Francisco. Each year, Tom O'Gorman, Pat Inman, and I travel with Cillian Purcell (our manager of regional operations) to every one of Gentle Giant's regional offices. Usually, we arrive in the evening and have dinner with the managers. The next morning, we gather everyone, early, before they head off to their first moves of the day. We join them on a run or on their version of the Harvard Stadium challenge. In San Francisco, for example, we sprint up the dunes of Thornton Beach. In Philadelphia, we run the length of Boat House Row, finishing up at the Art Museum, where we find our inner Rocky by charging up and down those famous steps. Afterwards, we sit down to a large breakfast, just as we do post-Stadium in Boston. And we talk to them about all the things I've described in this book. Our culture. Our values. How to connect with customers to better identify and fulfill their needs.

In the past, when we had fewer offices to visit and people to meet, we often had time to go out on the trucks with crews in other states. We still sometimes do that, although just for 30 minutes or an hour. It can be a memorable experience for the movers when they suddenly find me, the founder, on the other side of the armoire they are carrying. Some of them will suggest that Tom and I take it easy and offer to relieve us of a heavy load. We decline because we are there to remind our movers—wherever they live—that, at the end of the day, the Giants move people's goods. We are proud to do that. We love to do that.

As in Boston, a storytelling tradition flourishes in our branch offices. Managers there often relate tales of their exploits from their days in New England. They also describe superhuman movers and legendary crew chiefs who have been with us from the early days.

A Creative Friction—A Perfect Resolution

Doug Dietz, my stalwart partner, and numbers guy supreme, has guided us well. As a disciplined manager, he helped the company grow steadily. One of the ways we differ is that my tolerance for risk greatly exceeds his. Throughout the years, as we built the company, I tended to want to take flight, while he tended to ensure we stayed solidly grounded. You could say there was always this "creative" friction as we discussed each "next step." At a point when our remarkable success was beckoning towards becoming a much larger company, Doug approached me. He said he knew himself well enough to know that he wasn't the perfect CFO for the kind of larger enterprise we were becoming. Our original agreement was that if we dissolved the partnership, I would buy Doug out over four years. That's what happened. I was grateful and relieved when Doug offered to remain a Gentle Giant employee after he sold his shares to me. For the last 26 years, he has been our controller par excellence.

Leveraging Our Branches For Interstate Business

During our first 20-plus years, we did not do long-distance moves, but the list of repeat customers who wanted us to move them to other states kept growing. This growing list, along with our successful branch expansion, led us to view interstate moving as an irresistible opportunity. Having set up branches across the country, we were obviously well-positioned to become an interstate carrier. Although it may not be immediately apparent to those unfamiliar with the moving industry, being an interstate moving company differs in many significant ways from being a local moving company, even if the local moving company has branches in several different locations.

As previously explained, the interstate moving industry relies on contractors. Those contractors most often use hired casual workers.

While this is perfectly legal, it troubles me because these "casual workers" often work what amounts to a full-time schedule. Therefore, by my way of thinking, they should be entitled to the status of "employee" and be compensated as such. I was determined to do interstate the Gentle Giant way, with workers who have full benefits, are vetted, and are trained. By 2004, we had successfully established our New England branches and felt ready. Most of our drivers are former master crew chiefs with years of Gentle Giant experience.

With this decision to become an interstate moving company came the need for an in-house interstate expert to ensure everything was done properly and proceeded efficiently. I approached my friend Tom Anderson, who owned a very small local company, Saxon Movers, focused on interstate moving. He had just the right knowledge and experience. He and I were philosophically aligned—we are both avid in our commitment to the best interests of the customers. In 2005, we acquired Saxon, and our primary motivation was to bring Tom on board. It was he who led our interstate charge. In Gentle Giant interstate moves, the people who load and unload the trucks are all fully trained and insured professional movers with full benefits.

Jumping Through Hoops

Grappling with regulations is unavoidable for business owners. By the time you think about scaling, presumably you'll have done the work to comply with your home state. But every market you enter will present a host of fresh, sometimes unfathomable, regulations. We must become experts in these details because we must support our managers as they deal with all this infuriating red tape. Every industry has its own rambling assortment of regulatory headaches. Those that govern moving are especially onerous. In some markets, the process of getting a business license has been relatively straightforward; in others, nightmarish. And it's not as though you can figure out how to meet requirements and then apply what you learned to another city. Every new location has offered its own special twist. Each office opening is a new rodeo.

Of course, I understand that because we movers work inside people's homes, we must be closely scrutinized. I have been clear about how sensitive I am to the need to ensure the highest ethical standards for any employee I send into any person's home. I am very much in favor of any rules that are actually aimed at protecting the public. However, many of the rules struck me as emanating from legislative lobbying aimed at stifling competition. A good example of what I mean is the requirement in some states that new interstate applicants must demonstrate that the new market needs them.

In Pennsylvania, for example, it used to be that, if a set proportion of existing movers banded together to keep you out, then they could do just that. When we pursued a foothold there, they treated us like an invasive species. We had to solicit one resident from each of Pennsylvania's 63 counties who had used our services in the past to sign a petition supporting Gentle Giant in the state. We also needed an in-state mover to sponsor us. Imagine that! Hello, I want to set up my top-rated moving business down the street from yours. Can you help me make that happen? I could rest my case on this one example of a rule designed to block competition rather than benefit the public. But there are other examples. Portland, Oregon, where a similarly exclusionary process was in place, actually succeeded in ejecting us. A local lawyer persuaded 13 moving companies to join forces to keep us out. I heard that each one paid 1/13th of his fee. Our mistake was not hiring this guy ourselves first. (That was more than 20 years ago. Things have changed in Portland. We may take another crack at it.)

Some states, like North Carolina, California, and Washington, cap how much movers can charge. So much for free markets! It's a slap in the face for a company like Gentle Giant, which offers premium services and retains an all-employee moving force whose pay and benefits reflect our ethical business practices. Our margins are going to take a hit in places with those kinds of policies. But that doesn't mean we just roll over.

When you enter a new market, one of the first things to do is not just join, but become active in, the trade association for that state. At the Washington Movers Conference in Seattle, for example, we demonstrated to regulators that Gentle Giant and other companies were already performing every job at the maximum allowable rate. We provided them with data and broke down what that was costing us. Ultimately, we won a 22% increase in the price we can charge in that region.

Much of our success in navigating interstate regulations is due to Tom Anderson's insistence that we hire someone dedicated to compliance. Managing this minefield is a thankless task. The rules are so complicated and varied that people often find themselves in violation, even when they're doing their best to comply. Compliance professionals I knew seemed beaten down from all the wrist-slapping they had to do. I dreaded this particular job search. So, I was delighted to receive a letter from Lisa Rivard, who, after researching Gentle Giant, wanted to come work for us. Lisa had the perfect skill set for the job—a combination of a gracious temperament and attention to detail. She has become an invaluable member of our leadership team.

I must concede that, burdensome as we often find regulatory compliance, we've observed that some of the worst moving companies are in states with weak regulatory environments. I argue that regulation can work in your favor if you are supremely good at what you do. With the right people, like Lisa, overseeing compliance and putting in place the resources needed to meet, or, when appropriate, push back against, regulatory requirements, provides a competitive advantage. Competitors who fail to expend these resources struggle amid the morass of regulations. Then the risk of falling out of compliance becomes enormous. Even if regulators do not detect and cite violations, the quality of service and adherence to safe practices, inevitably, declines. As a result, companies like ours can become even more attractive to customers.

Growth Through Partnerships

With multiple offices, Gentle Giant has developed the experience and expertise to partner with quality local movers in regions where we're not represented. Our first such partner was Amazing Moves in Denver, run by two former Giants we know and trust. We have now set up partnerships with several companies. All have undergone an extremely rigorous vetting process. Our partners must follow Gentle Giant policies and practices: they must abide by our money-back guarantee, adhere to our hiring and training standards, and all their movers must be employees with insurance and benefits. One other issue of tantamount importance: All our partners must, just as Gentle Giant does, empower its employees to make decisions in the customers' best interest. Most moving companies require movers to obtain approval from headquarters before taking any action. We will never partner with a company wishing to follow such a policy. We do not compromise on this core principle: we ensure that customers receive the same quality of service from our partners as they do from us.

Gentle Giant deals with its partners in ways very similar to how we deal with our own expansion branches. For example, when we book interstate jobs with a partner, we pay them at the same rate their other customers are charged. That's a huge difference from what happens if they work with a van line. In that situation, for reasons reviewed previously, the local moving company is often forced to do jobs at a significantly discounted rate. Then, after the van line and the agent run away with the profits, the driver—an independent contractor who assembles teams at both ends—is left with about 60% of the fee to cover all costs, including their own pay.

The quality we offer requires charging a premium. This is the only way to ensure that every customer, everywhere, is served by employees who receive benefits, training, insurance—the whole package. Competing with a culture of discounts is tough. But we built our business on the belief that the way to put the customer first is to make sure we take proper care of the people taking care of our customers.

CHAPTER EIGHT

Using Giant HEART Values to Tackle Crises

A valued repeat customer stored some very expensive rugs at our storage facility. She always purchased insurance, but unfortunately, our movers forgot to tell her that, for the storage of valuable rugs, we require either that the rugs be professionally cleaned before storage or that she sign a disclaimer. Our movers had sealed her rugs in Tyvek to prevent contamination, but as it turned out, some of the rugs already harbored moth eggs.

Snug in their polyethylene terrarium, the insects hatched. When our customer saw the damage to a rug she had bought for $11,000, she broke down in tears. However, the rug expert hired by the insurance company valued that rug at just $4,000 because, he said, it was saturated with cat urine. That, he surmised, was what had attracted the moths in the first place.

Our quality control department was negotiating with the customer when I got a call from her boyfriend, a big-shot state official. "Our cats would never, ever, pee on a rug," he said. "They always use a litter box." He ranted that an incontinent racoon had infiltrated our warehouse.

I wanted to talk about this situation in-person, but, as I explained, I was leaving for Ireland that evening and would call him as soon as I returned. I assured him we were committed to a resolution that would make them happy. "What will make me happy is a check for $25,000. Right now."

(He was adding to the total the cost of two other rugs that needed some minor repairs.)

The following morning, I arrived in Ireland, jet-lagged, and planning to go to bed early. Before I turned in, I checked my e-mails. There was a message from the boyfriend's lawyer, curtly informing me that I was being sued for triple damages: $75,000. I was so upset I did not sleep a wink that night.

Upon my return, her boyfriend proposed excluding the customer from our meeting, but I insisted she be there. He set up the meeting at his office, a location that was very inconvenient for her. Predictably, she got stuck in rush-hour traffic. While we were waiting for her, he pressured me to propose my resolution to him, but I demurred. After an hour, our customer arrived and was characteristically gracious.

Since our deductible was $4,000, we would not receive any coverage from our insurance company. The most any other moving company would have paid out would have been the value as assessed by the insurance company ($4,000), and that was the extent of our liability. But our movers had erred by not following our policy of making sure the rugs had been professionally cleaned. Therefore, because of our Giant HEART value of going above-and-beyond for customers, I wrote a check for $11,000—the amount she had originally paid for the rug.

But I knew that the act of paying by itself would not be enough to shield Gentle Giant's reputation. Through the grapevine among Gentle Giant fans, I learned that her very prominent and influential boyfriend was badmouthing us. So, as I handed over the check, I asked for her assurance that he would proactively let people know we had done right by her. She assured me effusively that this would certainly happen. I was relieved to be able to stop an influential, disgruntled person from continuing to unfairly trample our reputation.

Keeping Calm and Carrying On

In the 1912 book *The Lighter Side of Irish Life*, the author advises that one has a much better chance of getting breakfast on time in an Irish hotel if there has been a flood in the kitchen the night before. The flood merely breaks the mundane routine. The opportunity to rise to the challenge is cherished. (Perhaps with tongue-in-cheek, the author contrasts Irish and English servants, claiming that the latter much prefer it when things run smoothly.) Solving problems under pressure energizes me and brings out my best. I am at ease in "flood-in-the-kitchen" types of events. I believe that being able to respond to unforeseen emergencies with this type of response is a great advantage, especially for anyone with entrepreneurial ambitions. In risky, uncertain environments, those who react to such challenges with enthusiasm rather than with fear or avoidance can thrive.

Crises will occur. People are going to make occasional serious mistakes. The most important thing I have learned on the job is to stay calm. No matter how bad things look, I don't get rattled. It comes naturally to me now. Keeping your cool is essential in a crisis, when you must think clearly, sift through new information, and make decisions quickly. Navigating a crisis is a nerve-wracking ordeal, and there is no "how-to manual".

On the other hand, crises can provide opportunities for truly extraordinary performance. This has certainly been the case for Gentle Giant. Making it through a crisis can position a company to emerge stronger.

I remember talking to my friend Gary Loveman when he was CEO of Caesars Entertainment. That company employed more than 80,000 people. He told me that every single day, at least one employee had to deal with a crisis—often one of tragic proportions. Talking to Gary helped put things in perspective. Bad things happen. The cause is often human error. Increasingly, there are cases of malware, technological malfunctions, and supply-chain snafus. In my world, customer disappointment resulting from damage triggers an emergency response. But, as discussed below, we have also dealt with many bona fide crises. Getting through them has taken ingenuity, grit, teamwork, and significant resources.

Other than incidents involving property damage, the most significant challenges I have faced include unforeseen accidents, financial crashes, and the 2020 pandemic (which shuttered many businesses). My values guide some of my reactions along with my innate personality. And how I have responded has evolved on the job as I've figured things out amid virtual storms.

I have now embraced some bedrock principles that guide me during crises. Vigilance and active listening usually enable us to head off trouble. Fundamentally, the best protection against an initial precipitating event or mistake spiraling into a crisis is strong policies that are universally understood and practiced. When employees are empowered to make decisions and know they should react calmly and in the customers' interests, they likely will be able to head off problems before they become crises.

Safety First

At every new-employee orientation, we ask our rookies, "What's the most important thing about moving?" The only correct answer is "Safety." Only about 20% get the right answer on the first day. But from that day on, everyone at Gentle Giant knows safety is our top priority. We do all we can to prevent any accidents.

When people are driving around in big trucks and hauling heavy loads up the sides of buildings, the potential for disaster is always present. As a company, we have had one very bad spinal injury. When it comes to crises, the only thing that would truly petrify me would be an accident that caused a death or serious injury. Brendan Ward, one of our great movers, suffered a serious injury in a freak accident in 2011.

I was devastated. I believe that if this accident had occurred a few years earlier—before so many people were dependent on the company—I would have shuttered the business. It took all the resilience I could muster to carry on. I believe what got me through this crisis was Brendan's very positive attitude and his refusal to feel sorry for himself. We all rallied to support him. Despite his devastating injury, he has built a successful life. Brendan is never far from my mind, and we do all that we can to prevent accidents. Whenever customers demand to speak to me and start ranting, as soon as I can get a word in edgewise, I ask: "Has anybody been hurt?" With the gruff acknowledgement of no injuries, I relax, and the customers generally start to see things in perspective. I can settle them down with the assurance that we will remedy the situation.

The best way to put yourself in a position to deal with a crisis is to adhere to clearly defined priorities. I am prepared, as all leaders should be, to move heaven and earth to make things right. This commitment springs automatically from our unwavering customer focused orientation—the basic requirement of a great service company. I always prioritize keeping things in perspective AND helping others keep perspective. And my perspective is guided by my core beliefs about how a service company should be run. Our priorities are: 1) the workers who provide the service and the people who provide the infrastructure supporting them; 2) customers; and 3) the bottom line. Putting the bottom line third is the best way to keep the company healthy and survive the test of time. Thank goodness we do not have stockholders, because their only focus is on short-term profits. When you have your priorities straight, you are well-positioned to handle crises.

Damage Avoidance

As a moving company, you expect crises—expensive or cherished heirlooms marred, damage done to someone's home, an accident involving a truck. But when we make a mistake (the seed of a crisis), there's consolation in the fact that we can correct it. Everybody knows human error cannot be completely avoided. We always keep in mind that taking great care of our customers' belongings is the essence of our business. We are honored that people trust us with their treasures. Our affluent customers (and we have many) consign near-museum-quality possessions to our care. Those kinds of jobs are often very lucrative but can have an expensive downside if something goes wrong. Thankfully, expenses of this kind are vanishingly rare at Gentle Giant because we train—and then retrain—exhaustively on the technical aspects of moving.

In a company that does tens of thousands of moves every year, the occasional significant snafu is inevitable. Reaching a settlement can be challenging if the insurance company denies a claim, or if there is no insurance and we judge that negligence has occurred, or if we decide to take care of something when there is no fault on our part. I learned the hard way that when a customer accepts a check, it does not mean that we have achieved resolution. Years ago, a customer accepted a settlement of $8,000 for a mistake that was not even our fault, and then continued to badmouth us.

This was a regretted expense, But, as demonstrated in the story that opens this chapter, the lesson learned was valuable. Before a check is handed over to a customer, the customer must agree that they will let people know that the situation has been handled to their complete satisfaction. Yes, snafus do happen. And when they happen, Gentle Giant works from the customers' perspectives to reach a resolution. Our Quality Control Department fully understands that there is no point in reaching a settlement with someone who, regardless of how well you have made amends, continues to trash your reputation.

The Irritation of False Accusations

Being accused of something you did not do is devastating. Honesty is the H in HEART, and at Gentle Giant, there has never been a theft. But, infuriatingly, when a customer cannot find an item after a move, they sometimes jump to the conclusion that a Giant must have taken it. It has always been that they eventually find it (exactly where they had forgotten they had packed it). When people call to tell me that my movers stole something, it gives me great peace of mind to know that they are mistaken. I stay relaxed, ask questions, and don't argue. For moving companies and contractors whose hiring decisions are not as rigorous as ours, it must be dreadful when such charges are leveled.

When customers express suspicions, there is little we can do beyond urging them to unpack each box and examine the contents carefully. But once a suspicion has entered the mind, it becomes hard to be open to other possibilities. When customers find whatever it is they suspected had been stolen, one of two things happens: they call to tell us and apologize, or they go radio silent. The way we know they have found the item is that our calls to them go unanswered and their phone calls to us stop.

A customer once accused a Giant of stealing a painting. We were aware that her husband had brought some of their artwork to their new home in his station wagon. But she refused to check whether the missing painting was among those still-wrapped pieces, even after we pleaded with her to do so. She was certain that her husband had not moved the painting in question.

I told the mover who was being accused that we knew he'd done nothing wrong. But he was crestfallen. Deciding to do some sleuthing of my own, I called the company that was remodeling the customer's new home. I told the story to the crew foreman and asked him to offer to hang her still-wrapped artwork. Surprise—there among them was the "stolen" painting. The customer ceased all communications and never called to acknowledge that she now had the painting hanging on her wall.

Thankfully, incidents of such atrocious behavior have been extremely rare. Examples of ethical behavior, on the other hand, are common. When one woman lost $22,000 worth of jewelry during a move, she sounded concerned and regretful rather than angry. Her crew had been so lovely. She couldn't imagine one of them had taken it, but she could think of no other explanation. Well, she eventually found the jewelry. And she was so contrite that she not only apologized but offered to take out a full-page *Boston Globe* ad to make amends in public. I was appreciative, of course, but told her I preferred she not spend her money in that way. Paying for such an ad would probably cost as much as her jewelry.

Financial Crises

Financial crises can persist for long periods, depress morale, jeopardize important projects, threaten the livelihoods of your people and—in the most serious cases—obliterate everything you've built. The larger the crisis, the more critical it is to remain calm and keep morale intact. In such high-stakes situations, anxiety within the workforce may be pervasive and almost palpable. The leader must respond with frequent, candid communication that neither sugarcoats nor unnecessarily alarms. You can't banish employees' fears, but sometimes they can use a leader's help when dealing with uncertainty.

In the early start-up phase of Gentle Giant, I believed the company was invulnerable to economic upheaval. Naively, I thought that we were protected because we had been built by word-of-mouth. My logic was that, even if business was down overall, people would still need to move. And when they did, they would choose their mover based on the advice of friends and relatives. Although across the market there would be less business, I figured we would continue to get enough business because people knew that Gentle Giant was by far their best choice. The early 1990s recession dispelled my naïve assumptions. During that period, many large moving companies went out of business or were sold. And I quickly learned just how tough the slow months can be in this seasonal industry.

At that time, we had not yet secured a line of credit with a bank. Doug came to me and said that the company was likely to run out of cash. The time was fast approaching when we would be unable to make payroll. I felt like a parent who suddenly learned he can't put food on the table. Word got around, as word does. Soon, all 12 of our salaried employees knew layoffs were imminent. Under such circumstances, one might predict that an "every-man-for-himself" atmosphere would invade. But all those years building employee trust and a teamwork culture really paid off. We had always done right by our people, and now, when we really needed them, they rallied to our aid.

Without telling Doug or me, the office staff held a meeting. Unanimously, they voted to propose across-the-board layoffs until our slow season had passed. They figured we could hold things together until then. They made a collective decision in the best interests of the business. The significant savings allowed us to eke by. This is the type of thing that is possible when management has earned the trust and support of the employees.

Relieved and grateful to have a plan proposed by employees rather than imposed by us, Doug and I readily agreed. Of course, moves were still happening. We had to maintain functions such as dispatch, sales, and quality control. In "flood-in- the-kitchen mode," I threw myself into the job—all 12 jobs, actually. Frantically, I called customers, movers, whomever we had to communicate with. In my conversations with customers, I discovered that a few of our laid-off employees had already reached out to them. To hasten our return to financial stability, they apparently were still doing their jobs—at least enough to keep us afloat. I didn't know whether this was appropriate or even legal. A labor attorney assured me that there was no legal issue if people were doing this on their own, without the owners' solicitation or approval. I felt a rush of gratitude for the sacrifices our people have made.

Mercifully, that was a short recession. We rebounded quickly. The 2001 recession was also short and shallow. By that time, we had a strong line of credit. Consequently, we managed a relatively smooth flight through the turbulence. Then came the Great Recession of 2008. In 2005, we acquired a building and lot in Somerville as our headquarters, and that had necessitated a substantial loan from our bank. The covenant stipulated that if, in any year of the loan, we failed to exceed 2% net profit, the bank could step in and order cutbacks and divestitures. Running the numbers in January 2008, we were horrified to find that we would close the year with a significant loss.

Again, our wonderful staff stepped up. After talking amongst themselves, they volunteered to take revolving furloughs. We also took advantage of a federal short-time compensation program that enabled us to lay off our entire salaried workforce for one day a week. Those employees could then collect unemployment for that day. The story of how we coped made the front page of the *Boston Globe*. Still, our combined efforts were not enough to reach the 2% net profit target. In fact, we were looking at a 2% loss. In June of 2008, I met with our bankers to explain that there was no way we would make our convenance.

"What do you think you can do?" they asked.

"I feel we can break even," I said, crossing my fingers behind my back.

To my relief, that answer didn't just satisfy them. They actually seemed pleased.

"That's better than most of our clients," they told me. "We are happy to change your 2008 convenance to breaking even. But next year, recession or not, your convenance will be back to 2%."

So, our folks did what they always do in a crisis: banded together and worked like hell. It didn't hurt that we had a fantastic new CFO, Ron Zahn, who helped steer us through those rough waters. In 2008, we eked out a profit of $40,000, pretty much the same as breaking even and enough to keep the Sword of Damocles from falling on our heads. This was the only year we did not meet our convenance.

The Pandemic—Everybody's Crisis

We cannot assume that the pandemic of 2020 will be the last. During a crisis of such epic proportions, when lives are on the line, protecting employees was Job #1. The pandemic had a catastrophic effect on many service businesses. In Massachusetts, the Governor declared a State of Emergency and ordered non-essential businesses to shut. After a few weeks of intense worry, as March 2020 drew to a close, we were declared an essential service and cleared to stay open. To our surprise, business kept pouring in.

The pandemic caused a great surge in the number of people who decided to move. Suddenly, millions were given permission to work remotely. Relieved of having to commute, many decided to relocate away from cities. Seeking social distancing, many decided to move out of apartment buildings and into suburban and small-town homes. We were fully booked.

We devised a plan to keep our people safe. We allowed our office staff to work remotely. We created a Covid-19 task force, run by Lisa Rivard, our Director of Compliance and Risk Management. For every job, we gave our movers kits with masks, gloves, and disinfectant. Employees reporting to work had their temperatures measured. We conducted daily Covid testing. If anyone tested positive, they and all who had recently worked with them were held back from work in accordance with Centers for Disease Control (CDC) guidance. Under these circumstances, staffing was extremely difficult. In addition, the government was paying people to stay at home. This was a great help to many of our employees who were living with elderly relatives or had young kids and were married to essential workers.

In those first few months, you'll recall, there was concern about spread from surfaces. We asked customers to wipe down surfaces with disinfectant. We switched out our furniture pads and disinfected the trucks every day. We knew we couldn't keep our people safe if customers didn't get on board with our precautions. Of course, we wanted customers to stay healthy, as well. So, we asked them to set aside a bathroom for our movers, who brought their own soap and washed their hands frequently throughout the job. We also required customers to always wear masks and to sequester themselves in a room or stay outside while the move was underway. Most complied without question.

In those rare instances when someone gave us a hard time, the crew chief warned that our people would climb back into their trucks and drive away. Once or twice, they did just that. But some of the less assertive crew chiefs ended up working with customers who, without masks, hovered over them while they worked.

At the time, there was a government-mandated paid leave program. To counter this, some companies offered an incentive to return to work. But I was dead set against doing that. If people did not feel safe coming to work, I did not want to incentivize them to do so. So, we muddled through with a skeleton crew. Our office staff filled in on the trucks as needed, as did Tom O'Gorman, our new CEO. Tom had assumed the top position in 2020. Almost immediately, he was splitting his time between working on the trucks and making the decisions that would determine our survival.

As a thank-you to those who worked during these dark days, after the fact, at the end of the month, we gave them a retroactive extra $4 per hour worked. Eventually, people who had stayed home started coming back to work. Although movers are, of necessity, an unusually healthy demographic, some of our crew members were over 50, a group deemed more vulnerable to serious illness by the CDC. This was before vaccines, and so we did not feel comfortable letting them return.

During that awful period, we managed to do some excellent work. For example, early on the city designated Harvard Medical School dorms as a location for hospitalized COVID patients. That meant the university had to relocate the medical students to Harvard Business School dorms. The medical school had a contract with another moving company, but that company was unable to complete the job. The school called us. Within two days, we had packed up and moved 250 students to their temporary housing, four miles away, maintaining strict COVID protocols throughout and freeing up space for the sick.

Our company and every one of our people survived the pandemic. I had feared that the pandemic might kill our business. It did not, and in fact, we provided a great and essential service throughout it. I'd like to think we've become experts at orchestrating moves in the middle of a global health crisis. It's an expertise I hope we will never again have to leverage.

Mulligan Management

Thank goodness we did not have a big crisis when Gentle Giant was small. That would likely have shut us down. For the first five years, I was never disappointed by anyone on my team. It was great to be surrounded by people who, if they made the occasional mistake, were able to correct it themselves. But then one day, one of my best crew chiefs made a mistake that neither he nor I could rectify. I erupted in anger because his mistake led a valued customer to vilify me—the only time this has ever happened. As the company grew, I occasionally encountered other mistakes, some of which precipitated crises. None rattled me to the same extent, but I always felt justified expressing some level of anger. It took me six years to realize how wrong I was.

Here is the story about that first angry eruption. A graphic artist booked a move that had to be loaded between 2 PM and 5 PM (the only time the elevator was available). I had personally moved this artist on two previous occasions, and I had a strong rapport with her. I booked a piano move for that morning, figuring there would be plenty of time to complete it before 2 PM. The two-man crew I dispatched for the piano job was led by one of my most valued crew chiefs. I scheduled a meeting with them for 2 PM regarding the artist's move.

When the crew on the piano move did not return when expected, I called their customer. She told me that the crew had delivered the piano and had done a great job. I therefore expected them back momentarily. I called the artist to reassure her that we were still on track to get her out of her building by 5 PM. But soon after 3 PM, instead of seeing the crew arrive in the yard, I got a call from the crew chief telling me the truck had broken down. That meant I would now have to rent a truck, bring it back to our yard, equip it, and arrange for a crew to meet me at the artist's building. By then it would be after 4 PM, too late to have her out of the building by 5 PM. I called to let her know. I apologized and offered to do the move for free. But she had trusted me to keep my promise to be there before 3 PM. This was, to her, a real betrayal by someone she considered a friend. She was very angry and told me that she wanted nothing further to do with me. I felt as though my heart had been ripped out. I had resolved never to deceive a customer, and now I was being accused of doing just that.

I was still extremely upset when I later saw the crew chief, I erupted in anger.

"God damn it!" I yelled. "If you had called me when the truck broke down, all would have been fine, and we could have avoided this mess."

I was like a raging bull. He explained that when the truck broke down, the customer had already left for her home. So he took the piano off the truck, strapped it to a dolly and pushed it a mile and a half to the destination. After delivering the piano, they had to carry all their gear, including a piano board, a stack of heavy pads, all their straps, tools, and a dolly more than a mile to a bus stop, and then take a series of buses to get back to our area.

The crew chief was baffled by my anger. He had performed heroically by marching that piano across the town of Arlington. This is a guy who, when he is on a move, has nothing on his mind except the job and the customer. And here I was, spewing anger at him. At the time, I was too angry to consider things from his perspective. Luckily for me, I had built up enough goodwill with him that he did not quit right then. He continued to work at Gentle Giant until his recent retirement. I was unmoved by the fact that this crew chief had made such a superhuman effort to take care of his customer.

It is embarrassing to admit how long I remained certain in the opinion that my angry response was appropriate. The first crack in this certainty came, I believe, from reading about leadership and the importance of modeling the behavior you want your people to emulate. I was also beginning to understand how the leader's words are amplified in employees' minds. Then, one day, I was confronted by a mistake far worse than the one described in the story above. Taken by surprise, I erupted in anger at the young mistake-maker. As this wonderful, good-natured, teddy-bear of a man was looking at me with confusion, I suddenly realized that my behavior, which in the past I had felt was justified, was in fact, misguided. Here was a young guy with the best of intentions. And I was screaming at him. I suddenly had an epiphany.

On the spot, I resolved never again to lose my temper. And for over 30 years, I've kept that vow. When a mistake causes a crisis now, I focus on the crisis, not the mistake. Later, when the heat is lower and the stress is off, there can be an adult conversation about what happened. The goal is not to blame, shame, or punish, but to make sure it doesn't happen again. I always reach deep for that empathy that will remind me to look at things from the other person's perspective.

This brings me to the vitally important concept of "Mulligan Management": When you have a first-class worker providing their best effort, it is never justifiable to get angry with them. There is always the possibility that highly valued team players, making their best effort, will make occasional thoughtless mistakes. When they do, you should give them a mulligan. You must find a way to address the issue without berating them. If you do slip-up and get angry, you should realize you are out of line and apologize. (And if you have people on your team who are not making their best effort, the person you should get angry with is yourself—because you are keeping them around.) Succumbing to emotions interferes with the intense focus required to solve difficult problems. Leaders should never hurl blame or lose their tempers. Doing so will undermine whatever goodwill has been amassed between a manager and their team. Mulligan Management has served me well for decades.

CHAPTER NINE

Giant HEARTs in the Non-Profit World

A repeat customer, a young woman named Kate, hired us to move her into her boyfriend's house. Doug and I did the job and finished it quickly. We wished Kate well in this new chapter of her life. Some months later, she called and said she needed to move in a hurry. Her boyfriend had become physically abusive. She told us not to arrive until after her boyfriend would be at work. But when we arrived at the appointed time, her boyfriend was standing in the driveway with Kate standing some distance behind him.

"Kate doesn't need you after all. You can turn around and leave."

That did not sound right to me. I hopped out of the truck and, to his astonishment, strode past him so that I could talk directly to Kate.

"Please get me out of here. Don't leave me alone with him," she whispered.

Doug and I started the job. The boyfriend followed Kate around, alternating between demanding and pleading for her to stay. But she kept close to me as I handed things to Doug, who was loading the truck. After a while, the boyfriend insisted he needed time alone with her.

"Give us some privacy," he said to me as if it was an ordinary request any couple might ask of a third party.

"Let me just grab these last few things," I replied as I continued removing items, with Kate following closely.

In the living room, as I picked up a table to take to the truck, the boyfriend positioned himself between Kate and me. His intent was obvious. He meant to close the door behind me as soon as I carried the item out. But the whispered entreaty that I do not leave her alone with him was on my mind. I placed the item on the other side of the threshold without leaving the room.

Then I retrieved the next item: an enormous armchair. As I maneuvered it through the doorway, the ex-boyfriend pushed me out into the hall and tried to slam the door shut. I threw back my foot and took the impact. Then I slowly pushed the door open as he shoved back against me. Given my strength, he might as well have been struggling with an elephant.

"Now I get it. You're just her hired thug!" he yelled.

I ignored him, but from that point, he redirected his ire towards me, following me around and berating me. I was relieved that he was no longer in Kate's face. Doug and I finished the job. We did not drive our truck out of the driveway until Kate had left.

That was my first experience with a move involving domestic violence. We have since done a lot of pro bono work in this area.

Service Companies to the Rescue

When Ben Franklin coined the phrase "do well by doing good," he seems to have kicked off the still-raging debate about the appropriate levels of corporate philanthropy relative to their impact on profits. My own view is that decisions on philanthropic activities should be guided by doing what we can to help, contingent, of course, on staying solvent and fulfilling our commitments to our customers, employees, and vendors. The way I see it, the company we have built is part of the community we live in. I am pleased when Gentle Giant can satisfy a community need. From my very early days as a mover, I have felt great satisfaction from what Gentle Giant has been able to do on a non-profit basis.

I am proud that my company is among the many service industries that routinely step up to meet the needs of a community. I don't think people realize how much these businesses do *pro bono*. When something catastrophic happens, often it's local businesses that come out strong, even though they're suffering too. After a natural disaster, restaurants will feed first responders and hand out food and other supplies to people in need. Hotels provide free rooms for evacuees. Contractors donate materials and labor to neighbors trying to rebuild.

And it's not just during emergencies that these businesses give back. Some laundromats offer free services for the homeless. Dry cleaners channel unclaimed business attire to newly released prisoners preparing for job interviews. Landscaping companies provide lawn care *pro bono* for the elderly and people with disabilities. Mechanics do free car maintenance for low-income families. All sorts of companies run fundraisers, blood drives, and toy collections.

Your average local business community is full of good neighbors. And they don't just donate their services; they also donate money. There's a report by SCORE, the national mentor network, that says 75% of small businesses donate, on average, 6% of profits to charity. It does not surprise me that businesses with deep roots in a local economy step up with concern and generosity to help meet the community's needs. Service companies are especially well-positioned to help their communities because their interactions with customers are, by definition, face-to-face. Gentle Giant's customers sometimes ask us to help others. For example, it was one of our customers who, as described previously, told us of the child prodigy in desperate need of a piano move.

Over the years, I have been warned that a reputation for doing *pro bono* work could attract people seeking to take advantage of us. The concern is that nefarious types might try to exploit us by pretending they are worse off than they really are. I tell them that I don't let occasional grifters alter my core values.

Gentle Giant Non-Profit Activities

It may not be obvious that there are many situations in which an individual or family is in trouble and needs help from someone with a truck and a good heart. It feels wonderful to think about all the ways we have been able to help. Our work touches people's lives so intimately that we can spot and, hopefully, address problems that companies operating out of office parks and factories cannot. Sometimes, caseworkers for social service organizations call and ask for our help. Often, the request comes from one of our own employees. Occasionally, a customer asks us to assist a friend or someone in his community who is in crisis. We don't say no to something like that. Our only requirement is that the work fits into our schedules.

Almost invariably, our movers are thrilled to do that kind of work. A few even ask, in vain, that they be allowed to forego their own pay. Movers have told me, 10 or 15 years after leaving Gentle Giant, that these experiences of helping those in need were extremely meaningful to them. When Gentle Giant employees, or any employees, find themselves scheduled for a *pro bono* move or see some of their colleagues do one, they get the message. They are working for a company that helps people. They are proud of that. And at Gentle Giant, those we serve *pro bono* receive service with the same HEART values as our paying customers.

Helping Individuals in Dire Need

I feel that delivering a service in person is more gratifying than paying someone else to do it. Two early examples of such service will always hold a special place in my heart—our work with the AIDS Action Committee, and what we did (and continue to do) for victims of domestic violence.

Larry Kessler of the AIDS Action Committee reached out to us in the mid-80s. They depended on Gentle Giant's services and generosity in that first decade of the AIDS epidemic. I recall our work for them with poignant sorrow. The disease was horrific. Fear and intolerance made things worse. Landlords were evicting sick people. Roommates were forcing them out. These patients were incredibly vulnerable. Housing insecurity made them more so. I went on the first of these jobs myself. I could tell that the home had once been lovely and well-tended. Now it had gone to rack and ruin. The resident was skeletal and borderline catatonic. He didn't seem like someone who should be moving. He seemed like he belonged in hospice care. By that time, I had already witnessed a lot of poverty and chaos. Lives that have been knocked off course by fate or failure. But this was on a whole other level. It was the first time I moved someone while holding back tears.

For our movers, working on those jobs was voluntary. A few opted out. They were the ones who had been duped by misinformation and worried about infection. Still, the majority would raise their hands eagerly whenever a move like that came up. I'm immensely proud of the teamwork that went into executing those jobs. Movers, sales, dispatch, and quality control all collaborated with exceptional care to ensure everything was done with sensitivity and respect.

As mentioned in the story at the beginning of this chapter, getting our customer, Kate, away from her abusive boyfriend was only one of many jobs involving domestic violence. Over the decades, Gentle

Giant has donated services to dozens of people in abusive situations at the request of charities that support them. Many of those escaping abusive relationships go directly to shelters, and of course those people cannot bring much with them. But after a while, the shelter may place them in an apartment somewhere. Then they need us to get their stuff. Whenever we get a job like that, even if there's a bit of hostility involved from an irate aggressor, our teams are eager to assist. We take precautions like those we took with Kate. We try to show up when the partner isn't home. We wear plain T-shirts and use a truck without our logo.

In some cases, instead of moving a victim's belongings, we will provide the furniture ourselves. We regard furniture cast off by our customers as an asset to be leveraged to help people in need. In a world full of people who don't have enough, or any, furniture, we find people who are happy to have the cast-offs from our other customers. Junk removal companies, who also get cast-off furniture, usually don't have appropriate warehouse space to store what they collect. They certainly do not have the logistical infrastructure needed to inventory and deliver what they collect. Anything they can't quickly sell will be sent to a landfill.

For a time, we partnered with an organization called Furnishing Hope, which helps move families out of homelessness and serves wounded warriors. We would take inventory of the furniture, which was mostly utilitarian goods: tables, chairs, and bureaus. Then we'd post the items on a website. Caseworkers who were assisting specific families would go to the site and allow the client to select what suited them. We would deliver it free of charge. That worked for a while. But things got a bit unwieldy because their organizational structure was incompatible with ours. They needed us to accommodate their delivery schedules, and our minimum requirement, as mentioned above, is that the *pro bono* client let us fit the job to our schedule. We are now partnering with Household Goods, a wonderful non-profit, whose organizational structure meshes perfectly with ours. They store the goods in their own warehouse. When they need help with a delivery, they'll call us. We do it for free.

Most people need moving services, regardless of their income. And while we associate poverty with not having things, the corollary is that what poor people do have, they need and most likely cherish. When they move, they don't have the option of just dumping their belongings with a junk service and buying new stuff for the new place. I remember a particular customer who booked a job, and I suspected he couldn't afford it. He lived in Central Square, my neighborhood at the time, so I decided to visit him before the move. The apartment was neat and tidy, and he clearly took pride in his home. His furniture was, to put it mildly, well worn. I couldn't see charging him.

"Look," I said, "I'm more than happy to move you for free."

"I've worked hard to afford this," he replied. "I'm going to goddamn pay for it, whether you like it or not."

He proceeded to tell me his life story: about how he had survived homelessness and struggled to get back on his feet. I did the move with Tommy Pendergast, one of our early Giants. He could not believe I was charging this person, so I explained the situation to him. Afterward, while we were getting lunch close by, Tommy said he had to make a phone call. When he returned, he very happily told me he had convinced the customer to accept his wages from the job as a gift. I can only speculate that the customer accepted Tommy's contribution because he was too gracious to refuse it.

Although Gentle Giant still does the occasional free move as a one-off, for the last couple of decades, most of our *pro bono* work has been in partnership with charitable organizations. We are a natural go-to for non-profits dealing with homelessness and shelter issues. Those helping people in vulnerable living situations come to us for help just as soup kitchens rely on restaurants for donations and volunteer cooks.

Servicing Non-Profit Organizations

Charitable organizations themselves often need our services. Perhaps they are relocating their headquarters or expanding into new offices. Depending on the size of the job, we might do it *pro bono* or charge only for labor. We deliver goods collected by charitable organizations to local food banks. We are proud that so many moving companies support Move for Hunger, a non-profit organization that works with the transportation industry to reduce waste and hunger. In 2021, Gentle Giant won their "Mover of the Year Award." In that year alone, we delivered roughly 400,000 pounds of food.

As the years have gone by, we have continued to discover many ways our trucks and people can serve. Often, we volunteer for civic and fundraising events, such as parades, regattas, and marathons. Attendees will buy food from the stands and sit in the bleachers. Do attendees ever wonder what all the setup looked like? Or about who makes it disappear afterward? In cities where we operate, the answer is often: "Gentle Giant does."

Our trucks have also come in handy during natural disasters. After Hurricanes Katrina and Sandy, we announced that we would transport donations to victims. Religious leaders in the affected areas told us who in our region was collecting food, clothing, medicine, toiletries, and other supplies. Our crews picked everything up and then hit the road. Usually, we'd just deliver the donations to a religious or charitable organization at the other end. Once during Sandy, though, the church in Rockaway Beach was so overwhelmed that our people had to handle the distribution. When an earthquake devastated Haiti in 2010, Gentle Giant collected donations for the victims. We turned over two truckloads of crutches, wheelchairs, and other medical supplies to Partners in Health, a local nonprofit that delivered the aid. Over the years, we have also helped by retrieving laboratory equipment from companies going out of business and storing it in our warehouses. Partners in Health has then had us send the equipment as needed.

There is a great non-profit here in Boston called More Than Words. It takes in donated books and trains inner-city youth to run a couple of bookstores. This helps them to build skills and self-sufficiency and eventually to embark on sustainable careers. Over the years, we have donated hundreds of thousands of books accumulated from customers who decide not to move them to their new homes. Collecting books for More than Words is one of our most rewarding endeavors.

Because we are a physical and competitive bunch, our people are forever signing up to do bike-a-thons, walk-a-thons, marathons, and every other a-thon you can imagine. We routinely pledge to each of those challenges. Once in a while, a special project comes along that speaks to our culture of athleticism and determination. For example, we helped fund a documentary about Andrea Lytle Peet, a triathlete who, to my knowledge, is the only person with ALS to complete a marathon. Using a recumbent tricycle, she went on to complete marathons in all 50 states, all while raising $750,000 for ALS research. There is no way that Gentle Giant would have turned down the opportunity to put its name and money behind this story. Across the country, our managers have continued the Gentle Giant philanthropic traditions. They have offered support and *pro bono* services for everything ranging from religious charitable organizations to Pride events. It helps employees feel connected to their communities.

The Gentle Giant Charitable Foundation

In 2005, we established the Gentle Giant Charitable Foundation. It became our vehicle for contributing to and partnering with organizations dedicated to youth development. I've always believed that most social ills—alcoholism, petty crime, drug abuse—are so intractable because our young at risk people do not get the help they need. You have to get in there when kids are quite young and help them learn about how to choose the right path.

Our first initiative started around 2001, before the formal establishment of our foundation. We got involved with Read to a Child, a national literacy and mentoring group. In addition to company donations, many of our employees began visiting a local elementary school on Tuesdays during lunch to read to students. The foundation has also worked with Bunker Hill Community College in Boston.

A major recipient of our funding is the Gentle Giant Rowing Club, launched around the same time as the foundation. Over time, the company has donated close to half a million dollars. Rowing helped me build confidence and character—but it is an expensive sport not readily available to inner-city kids. The Gentle Giant Rowing Club aims to change that. Hundreds of young people, both male and female, have participated. The club has provided opportunities, similar to those I had as a young person, to learn the value of teamwork, develop discipline, build confidence, and enjoy the social camaraderie of a shared endeavor. Many of our club participants have gone on to success at the college level and beyond. Where possible, Gentle Giant branches in other cities have also supported rowing activities for young people. Our Philly office, for example, sponsors events with Philadelphia City Rowing. This organization combines academic support and other services with a structured athletic program to develop local high school students.

Spontaneous Samaritan Moves—Just for the Fun of It.

Not every generous act has to be a grand, noble gesture. It can be a lot of fun to lend a hand (along with our strong backs and Giant HEARTs). Gentle Giant's Roving College Moving service, which operated as a scheduled activity in the mid-2000s, is now performed spontaneously at the discretion of individual crew chiefs. It is a playful tradition very much in the spirit of the company. The fundamental idea is that crews descend unexpectedly on amateurs struggling to move heavy stuff. They move difficult items as a surprise favor.

The Boston area provides the perfect conditions for these "Spontaneous Samaritan Moves." During the few days around August 31, hundreds of thousands of students descend on the Boston area to start the college year. U-Hauls and minivans square off against each other in the streets. Cars double-park. Boxes are piled on sidewalks. Parents and students struggle to move heavy items (boxes, heavy furniture, etc.) from rented trucks to walk-up dorm rooms or apartments.

With this reliably predictable mayhem, everybody in the area who can avoid moving during this time does so, leaving us with lots of small jobs, sometimes with time between them. Driving through the mayhem, crews who spot beleaguered parents wrestling with mattresses, couches, and other large items, can, if they wish, leap from trucks and assist in the move. In just a couple of minutes, the parents and students are delivered from what had seemed like an eternity's worth of labor.

What a blessing! While driving from job to job, movers who find themselves in student-dense areas keep an eye out for those who appear to be in obvious need of help. When the Giants swoop in, people are surprised and delighted, and this gives us great satisfaction. Our reputation gets a big boost, some college kid has a story for life, and our movers have a blast.

I am proud to say the "Spontaneous Samaritan Moves" was my idea. I was the first to do them. I felt the way I imagine a standup comic must feel after a joke lands and laughter ensues. I remember one dad calling after me, "Who was that masked man?" To which my crew member yelled back, "He's the Gentle Giant!" If only I had had a cape.

My Next Giant Step

I am very pleased that Gentle Giant has been able to help so many different people in so many ways. Now that I am semi-retired, I want to focus on the issue that is most important to me. I believe that global warming is a threat to humanity. Among the many challenges being addressed by myriad foundations aimed at helping humanity, this one looms the largest for me.

For that reason, Gentle Giant is helping to found a nonprofit we have named REACH GREEN (reachgreen.org), aimed at raising money to preserve and expand green spaces and to fight climate change.

REACH GREEN was created to bring more people into the climate action movement, especially those connected to outdoor spaces through their daily activity. 242 million Americans engage in outdoor activities tied to green spaces. But green spaces, essential to sport, well-being, and community, are under direct threat, with outdoor activities impacted by higher temperatures, air quality declining due to wildfires, less snow, torrential rains, and floods.

REACH GREEN is being developed as a nonprofit platform that will mobilize endurance athletes, outdoor enthusiasts, and community-minded individuals to protect and preserve green spaces through movement, membership, storytelling, education, and partnerships.

We won't replace the organizations doing restoration and advocacy work. Our goal is to support and amplify them. As we grow, we aim to direct resources to a mix of national partners and local environmental organizations doing high-impact work in the places our community cares about.

CHAPTER TEN

Charting the Path Ahead

One day, the dispatcher got a call from a crew chief who said he had just left a job before he had even begun it.

"We can't do this move," he said. "There is junk piled to the ceiling in every room. I have explained to the customer that she needs to hire a junk removal company to remove the piles of trash and junk before we can load our trucks. She wouldn't listen to me and told me I was being ridiculous. She wants everything loaded onto our trucks."

The dispatcher, who at that time thought he had seen everything, was astonished by the photos sent by the crew chief. Junk and trash were indeed piled up to the ceiling in doorways, and one could not even tell what furniture might be behind, or on top of, the junk.

"I cannot ask my crew to do this move", the crew chief continued. "There are cats living among the debris and, despite that, there are rat droppings all over the place. I don't know how her kids have been able to survive. I have apologized and said we cannot do the job. I am sorry to report that I am returning to base with the three trucks and 5 crew members that you assigned to this job."

The crew chief was following Gentle Giant policy. Our employees are never expected to do any job that they perceive would jeopardize safety. In fact, they are expected to do as this crew chief had done—politely decline to proceed. The dispatcher relayed the crew chief's decision to upper management. A short time later, a call came in from a priest who wished to intercede on behalf of the customer.

Tom O'Gorman, VP of Sales, took the call. The priest explained that this family was in desperate straits. He acknowledged that the mother had spiraled into a dysfunctional state. He explained that a family member was stepping in to rectify the horrible situation, but that plan depended on getting them out of that house. They needed to be moved, regardless of the mother's inability to perceive how extraordinarily horrible her living conditions were.

Tom knew that a crew of six men had already determined that the job was unsafe, unsanitary, and beyond what could reasonably be expected of employees. He decided there and then that he would clear his calendar, call for volunteers to crew with him, and be the crew chief on the job himself. He assured the priest that this family, which was obviously dealing with a dire mental health crisis, would receive all the help they needed from Gentle Giant. He did the job over three days with three trucks, bringing seven different movers each day. With this arrangement, he was the only crew member who would have to tolerate these conditions for more than one day.

It was a surreal scene, made even more surreal by the customer's perception of the situation as normal. Eventually the crew "bush-whacked" their way to the room of her teenage son. He was a computer gaming addict, and he had bottles of urine lined up near his desk. He was cheerful and friendly and he, too, acted as if the situation was completely normal.

Halfway through the second day, the crew got its biggest shock. They opened the door to the preteen daughter's room. Her room was clean, tidy, and well organized! This young girl was managing to cling to normalcy amid all the dysfunction and hoarding surrounding her. Until this point, our movers had approached this job by calling on their HEART values of respect and non-judgement. Upon finding the girl in her room, they felt a sense of surprise, joy, and purpose. They were going to be heroes for this little girl.

Tom had taken the priest's word that the intervening family member would pay the bill. Sure enough, he left with a check for over $20,000. Tom is the kind of leader whose empathy and compassion brings the same out in his crew, and he had no trouble finding volunteers for each day of this uber-challenging move. Working with so many like-minded, empathetic people has led Tom to love this company and to commit to spending his career with us.

Take the Money and Run? No Thanks

When I was in my fifties, I began the process of figuring out how best to preserve this legacy and secure the future of Gentle Giant. During this long process I have been faced with many thought-provoking choices. Now I am enjoying a sense of contentment— confident that the decisions I have made are best suited to the Gentle Giant legacy, the company's future health, and my own personal goals.

Starting around 2000, I was bombarded with proposals from people who hoped to get rich by helping me get rich. They reached out about buying my business, helping me sell it, and advising me on how to invest the money I would receive from such a sale. Others pushed franchising as the most lucrative option.

When I look at the awful decisions made by companies, I see them driven by the imperative to maximize short-term profits. Public companies, in particular, do bad things in the interest of creating shareholder value. Even when they succeed financially, you can watch as their principles evaporate. Over the years, I have seen this scenario play out repeatedly at service companies around the country. I would not let it happen to Gentle Giant. True, I could make a lot of money if I sold Gentle Giant. But the company's success was not my success alone. It was the collective success of generations of committed and caring employees. For them, I was determined that this company would stand the test of time.

Back around 2010, as I approached 60, I was inundated with offers from people involved in mergers and acquisitions who were eager to make money by helping me make money through the sale of Gentle Giant. I ignored all of them. But one day, one of my movers, whose dad was, I already knew, involved in the M&A game, told me his dad wanted to meet with me. It would have been rude to ignore this request.

As luck would have it, the family was moving, and of course, they had booked Gentle Giant. I love to show up and talk to customers while moves are in progress, so I drove out to meet the dad on move day. As I expected, he told me that when the time came for me to sell, he would love to help me maximize my return. I explained that I was not interested in selling and that I already had a successor in mind. Then he played the tried-and-true-trump card—the one that often triggers start-up entrepreneurs to sell:

"What if something happens to you and the company flounders. Your wife will be left with nothing."

"That's not a concern," I said, "she is on board with me in this. Besides, she would not welcome the stress of figuring out where to donate all that money."

And I was being absolutely serious when I said that. I should also mention that my wife, Joan Karpinski, has always been 100% supportive of me. She has been the perfect person to bounce new ideas off and she has helped me navigate many difficult decisions. His best argument having failed to sway me, he tried an appeal to personal vanity and materialism.

"Play it safe," he said. "Sell now, pocket millions, and swap out that Prius for a Ferrari."

"Gentle Giant is my Ferrari!" I informed him.

"When someone drives your Ferrari into a ditch," he responded, "you'll be left with nothing."

But I wasn't worried about that. You see, I already had my Michael Schumacher.

It went without saying that the next CEO of Gentle Giant would be wholly committed to what we do and how we do it. A person intimately familiar with every gear and lever of the business. A leader who already commanded the trust of employees and could take my place with minimal disruption. My path forward had become clear—protect my legacy, my employees, and my customers by delivering it into the hands of the right successor.

Up from Reception

Gentle Giant thrives on employee referrals, and I generally interview those candidates out of courtesy. You never know who will present themselves. In 1994, a guy walked through my door. He was in his early 20s, with hair to his waist, wearing a leather jacket, and toting a motorcycle helmet. It was the slow season, and we really weren't looking to hire anyone. So, I thought to myself: "this shouldn't take long."

The previous year, Tom O'Gorman, right out of college, had emigrated from Ireland to the United States. That first summer, he'd worked on Cape Cod: waiting tables and doing landscaping jobs. He was a college friend of Briain Coleman, a mover who now manages operations at our Charlestown office. Briain—as hundreds had done before him and thousands more would do after him—recommended that his friend check out Gentle Giant.

Tom was applying for work on the trucks. I asked him,

"What do you hope to get out of this job?"

"I'm looking for a home," he replied.

That simple sentence spoke to me. This person didn't just want to work for us. He hoped to find a place that he could commit to and would commit to him. If what Briain had told him about us was true, he wanted to be one of us.

That routine job interview evolved into an intense, three-hour conversation. In almost everything Tom said, he appeared to me to epitomize what we always look for. People talk about the importance of culture fit. Tom and the Giant culture seemed custom-made for one another. I remember thinking, "I must make it so that this person never wants to leave."

That interview took place during a recession and as we were entering our slow season. At the time, I had no work for Tom on the trucks. But I wasn't going to let someone of his caliber twist in the wind. Fortunately, we had just hired a new receptionist who couldn't start for a week. That meant we had no one at the front desk. Tom jumped at the chance to fill in.

The next day, I was out on the trucks when my pager went off. It was Nancy Andrie, our office manager. I realized I'd forgotten to tell her about Tom and began apologizing, assuring her he was only temporary. But Nancy interrupted me. "That is not why I'm calling you," she said. "This guy is gold. Can we un-hire the new receptionist?"

As luck would have it, a family situation prevented the receptionist from ever starting with us. Tom was off and running. In everything he did, Tom had that golden touch. On the reception desk, he would respond to several calls simultaneously, handling each with aplomb. After a few months, Nancy suggested moving him to sales. "You will not believe what this guy is going to do," she predicted. Tom started in sales that May and closed $100,000 in business. It was double the previous record for a single month.

But Tom wasn't obsessed with his own stats. His priority was that the entire team succeed. So many sales cultures suffer from unhealthy competition. But Tom was completely unselfish, always supporting his coworkers. Everyone took a shine to him. At the same time, he continued to perform brilliantly on his own, bringing in between $2 million and $3 million a year. Part of that was talent. Part was his work ethic. And part was his drive to take care of people.

I saw that Tom could play a huge part in our future. I wanted to give him a range of experiences. After a few years, I offered him the operations manager position. The promotion meant more money and authority. Most people would have leaped at the opportunity. But Tom demurred. He wasn't ready, he said, because he hadn't spent enough time on the trucks.

Like many of our office staff, Tom had done moves periodically during peak periods. But he didn't think that he had enough experience. Tom had enormous respect for our crew chiefs and felt that, before he could lead them, he should first rise to their level. If I needed further proof that Tom understood, viscerally, what this company was all about, that protestation was it. I have always believed that serving shoulder-to-shoulder with front-line workers is among the best uses of my time—and the time of any service-company CEO. That's how you keep your finger on the company's pulse. That's how you build respect and loyalty with employees.

Once Tom had spent more time on the trucks, we moved forward to shift him to operations. Doug could not believe I was taking Tom out of sales. "You have signed the death warrant of this company," he warned. But I believed the positive changes in the sales team Tom had nurtured would be sustainable in his absence. Turns out, I was right.

Large corporations routinely rotate leadership candidates through senior positions in multiple departments. In the early to mid-2000s,

Tom was progressing through Gentle Giant's version of all the company milestones. After several years in operations, he became vice president of sales. He excelled there, as in every previous position.

I was already imagining Tom at the top of the company, carrying on what I had started while also making it his own. I had so much faith in and respect for him that I knew whatever future he created would enrich our legacy. But one question remained unresolved. I had no idea whether Tom even wanted to be CEO. In 2010, I asked the question. Tom did not hesitate. His eyes lit up and he enthusiastically accepted.

At that point, I was 59. Tom was 39. I decided that I would step down in 10 years. That meant I could breathe easy for five years before beginning a five-year transition. Recognizing the importance of a gradual, intentional process, I felt five years was the perfect amount of time.

Protecting The Legacy

Having got to the point of realizing I had an obvious successor, I turned my attention to how to make a graceful exit. My ability to do so was enabled by two strengths that already existed within the company and should exist within all great companies. The first strength involves talent. Leaders must be connoisseurs of potential: able to recognize it. And they must be interested enough in their people to get to know them. That goes for everyone, even the most junior employees. The current CEOs of several major corporations started at their companies by unloading delivery vehicles, working on assembly lines, operating elevators, working in mail rooms, or answering phones at reception. That last position produced the chief executives of Planet Fitness, the advertising behemoth Hill Holiday—and Gentle Giant.

The ability to spot great promise should be nurtured in every person who has anyone who reports to them. All executives and managers must understand that their jobs aren't just about developing people to do great work in the present. They also must figure out who will replace them in their own jobs in the future. The most important act of mentorship is preparing a successor. The process should be both gradual—ideally unfolding over several years—and intense. The assistance and support of everyone in the company should be sought. Engaging outside expertise should be considered.

The second strength involves what I have described as our values and culture of teamwork. Everything done to embed the company's values, behaviors, and standards helps guarantee a brilliant succession. Those who have thrived and risen to the top in our value-driven environment have, as far as I am concerned, identified themselves as the obvious bearers of our legacy.

Finding my new CEO has left me free in ways I haven't felt for decades. For me, it has meant a more focused effort on philanthropy. Founders whose identities are, like mine, intertwined with their companies will likely hang around for a while. This should be a good thing. The wisdom and institutional memory they provide, together with the respect and affection they engender, are valuable assets. But remember, someone else now stands at the helm. Step back and let that person steer the ship. In making my exit from the role of CEO, I accomplished my objectives of minimizing disruption, preserving and expanding on what I had built, and staying involved.

Home-Grown Talent

When you grow to a certain size, conventional business wisdom holds that you need new leadership with experience in the larger size business. I don't go along with this thinking. Why would I recruit from elsewhere when I have developed my own employees as my business has grown? The desire for home-grown leaders is one reason we've invested so much in coaching and training. We're not putting all this money, time, and energy into people just to replace them with off-the-rack MBAs from companies I do not wish to emulate. We want our home-grown talent to lead our company.

The prospect of advancement also keeps good employees in place. Because our employees know that all our managers have come up through the ranks, they realize those positions are within reach. To get ahead, though, they must embody our values. The great benefit of the "up-through-the-ranks" system is that you always get managers and executives who consistently demonstrate the Giant HEART.

However, when executive teams are drawn exclusively from in-house talent, a vigilant guard against certain types of pitfalls must be maintained. For example, people who have worked together for a long time may become so friendly and perhaps like-minded that they cease to challenge each other. They could start to fall short on their feedback-giving responsibilities. Longstanding dynamics—for example, comfortable deference—could settle in. At Gentle Giant, we are determined to avoid these potential pitfalls. We remain assiduous about team makeup, balance, and management. Our training in feedback and speaking up with respect must never wane. Unhealthy relationships rarely start anywhere in the company, and we vigilantly guard against them. But doing things the in-house way requires getting it right from the outset. New blood isn't necessary if your tested, trusted, devoted, and deserving blood is healthy. All members of our executive team are people who joined at an entry-level position and rose through the ranks.

One thing conventional business wisdom does get right is that succession planning should be happening all the time. And not just at the top level. Everyone in my leadership team is responsible for mentoring someone who could replace them. Adrian Farrell came onboard in 1996. Like Tom, he started on the reception desk and as a part-time mover. Then he joined Doug in finance. From 2000 to 2007, he worked with Phillip Green, our CFO. In 2008, Ron Zahn became our second CFO.

When I hired Ron, he was 10 years shy of retirement. From the start, part of his mandate was to get to know Adrian and take his measure. Ron told me he saw the same amazing qualities in Adrian as I did. "Great," I said. "Your job is to turn him into a top-flight CFO." Which is exactly what Ron did. I also told Ron to inform me if, for any reason, he did not think Adrian would work out in that role. When you ask leaders and managers to mentor specific successors, they must be candid in their observations of those people. They shouldn't worry they'll be blamed if the boss's choice can't get up to scratch.

Thinking about Tom, Adrian, and other future leaders of this company gives me confidence. Today may be the first day at the reception desk or on the trucks for some young man or woman who will eventually succeed Tom as CEO. In fact, Tom's contract requires that, when his time to leave comes, he identify a successor from within the organization rather than sell to an outsider. You can't guarantee the future, but we should do what we can to lay the groundwork for building the future we want.

Smooth Pass of the Baton

In the weeks after I announced that Tom would be the successor, people everywhere congratulated me on my choice. The prospect of being led by him reduced anxiety about an anticipated critical transition. The best way to prepare someone to be a CEO is to have them hold the role in tandem with them as much as possible. That's not the same as shadowing, which implies one person is more substantial than the other. Tom started out by joining me on daily schedule. At meetings, we shared the (metaphorical) podium. Increasingly, Tom would take the lead. He also accompanied me on trips to our offices around the country. There, the local teams came to know Tom as my peer.

Because I'm passionate about the people aspect of this business and my aptitude in connecting with people, HR or managers would occasionally ask me to help resolve personnel issues. (While this is an unusual role for a CEO, my belief is that the culture of the company should allow for "an open-door policy" when someone needs specific guidance.) Tom took over this role. He would arrive at a solution and then come talk it through with me. Invariably, I admired his decision-making skills. My confidence in him continued to expand

Because the succession process was so crucial, I sought outside assistance. Bonni Carson DiMatteo, the president of Atlantic Consulting, had assisted us with previous leadership projects. She helped me create a schedule to hand off specific responsibilities to Tom. We determined what experiences and skills he needed, for example spending time with our CFO to get a handle on the financial picture. Once he'd mastered an area, we'd move on to the next one.

An initial concern about Tom was that he might be too nice. Some expressed worry that he might be a pushover. He listens, is always cordial, and he works to understand the other point of view. He is very good at building consensus and can be very persuasive when he needs buy-in. Tom has repeatedly demonstrated that his kindness does not diminish his effectiveness. When decisiveness is needed, whether in a personnel or other situation, Tom takes action.

On the matter of ownership, we decided that the company would finance Tom's buyout of 51% of the shares. Over 20 years, he would pay me back. I would retain 30% of Gentle Giant, with the remaining 70% divided among three vice presidents to whom I had earlier awarded equity. This arrangement is common in family businesses (where it benefits the owner's son, daughter, or other relative), but is unusual in my type of situation.

Some have questioned why I didn't make Tom CEO and sell the business outright. But sooner or later, the new owners might replace him, putting at risk all we have achieved. I'm well aware that most owners wouldn't do things this way. And I would never be the judge of an individual who secured a hard-earned payout upfront. In April 2020, I formally ceded the CEO title to Tom. For me, this was the right solution, and I am resting easy with it.

Tom Succeeds, I Sustain

Like many people who love their work, I'm not sure I'll ever step away entirely. My title now is president. My objective—a good one, I think, for any founder who has moved out of the top executive slot—is to remain involved without being intrusive. Though I am no longer CEO, I will always be the founder. I derive satisfaction by serving as our company's ambassador and by teaching about Giant HEART values. I visit our field offices to support the Giant culture as it spreads across the country and reinforce the message that we are one team. I run alongside the new recruits at Harvard Stadium. Tom attends the orientation presentations on our Giant HEART values I give after these workouts. But I still deliver most of these myself. There are some things I can't quite give up.

I'm so grateful that I can relinquish leadership to a new generation while holding onto many aspects of the job I love. Maybe that's what founders should strive for as they recast relationships with their successors—to be wanted and not needed. I don't think I'm a very different person from the rower who, back in the '80s, bounded up and down stairs and coaxed 600-pound pianos around impossibly tight corners, all with a smile on my face. But in the years since then, I have learned a great deal about leadership.

The time is long gone when I let my emotions rule the day. I am more patient and approachable. I know I don't have all the answers. I solicit other people's ideas and opinions. I have learned to always listen and how to listen. The Giants are always happy to see me and show appreciation for what I've given them: respect, encouragement, opportunity, and this company. Gentle Giant truly does belong to every one of us.

Now you know my story. As a young man I started Gentle Giant on my own and almost by accident. I take great pride in what it has become. I am writing this book, in part, to acknowledge and thank all the amazing Giants who have contributed to an audacious experiment that became such a remarkable success. I am very lucky to find myself in a company that brings me boundless joy, created by my total confidence in every single crew we send out to our customers.

For decades, running Gentle Giant has given me the high runner's feel when, halfway through a marathon, they have the confidence they will finish strong. I am determined that the Giant HEART will continue to win customers' hearts, and that the company will continue to equip people with the skills to lead fulfilled lives.

Larry O'Toole and Tom O'Gorman

Acknowledgements

First and foremost, let me thank the myriad stalwart movers whose consistent hard work, enthusiasm, and Giant "HEARTS" helped build the company into what it is today. Thanks to my great friend, Hugh Norton, for convincing me to give moving a try, and to Doug Deitz, whose business and organizational skills ensured that Gentle Giant was built on a strong foundation.

Every leader has moments of self-doubt. I am so grateful to Nancy Andrei, Kathy Harny, Nicole Wolf, Bambi Banchongmanie, Danielle Rankin, and my sister, Jackie, for their unwavering encouragement and support.

The saying that writing and publishing a book is a marathon and not a sprint is very true, and I'm thankful to Ken Lizotte CMC Emeritus and Elena Petricone of emerson consulting group, inc. for all their help in getting the book over the finish line. Thank you for believing in the heart and soul of this book and for being my faithful publishing partners.

A thousand thanks to my wonderful wife, Joan Karpinski. My deepest gratitude goes to my sister, Margot, for her belief in Gentle Giant and for her conviction that this book should be written. With her editorial expertise, the Gentle Giant story is now in your hands. I hope you enjoy reading it as much as I enjoyed living it.

About the Author

Larry O'Toole moved to Boston, Massachusetts, from Ireland with his family when he was 15. He attended Northeastern University, where he developed a passion for rowing. Upon graduation, he pursued a career in engineering. His work experiences in manufacturing led him to realize he wanted to start his own business.

Larry founded Gentle Giant with a single business plan. "Only hire nice people with winning personalities and a strong work ethic, who are intelligent, physically fit, and have a passion for service." In other words, hire the kind of people you would relish spending a long, hard day working with. He likes to say that it was an experiment. Would that alone lead to success? It turns out that it did.

Larry and his wife, Joan, live in Andover, Massachusetts, with their Irish Water Spaniel Brogie, who appreciates swimming in the ponds of Harold Parker State Forest.

About Gentle Giant Moving Company

Founded in 1980 by Larry O'Toole, Gentle Giant Moving Company has grown from a single truck in Somerville, Massachusetts, into one of the most respected moving companies in the United States. With headquarters in Boston and regional offices across the country, Gentle Giant is known for delivering a stress-free moving experience and exceptional customer service.

Gentle Giant has set the industry standard through its dedication to customer trust and commitment to training and developing professional movers. Its workforce includes many former collegiate athletes, a nod to the company's rowing heritage and its emphasis on endurance, discipline, and teamwork.

Over the decades, Gentle Giant has earned national recognition for excellence in service and workplace culture. The company has received numerous awards for quality, leadership, and innovation, while maintaining a reputation for integrity and community involvement.

To learn more about Gentle Giant Moving Company, visit **www.gentlegiant.com**

www.ingramcontent.com/pod-product-compliance
Lightning Source LLC
LaVergne TN
LVHW010656110826
845149LV00014B/3120

9798995508809